How Bush and Ashcroft Have Dismantled the Bill of Rights

ELAINE CASSEL

Lawrence Hill Books

Library of Congress Cataloging-in-Publication Data

Cassel, Elaine.
    The war on civil liberties : how Bush and Ashcroft have dismantled
the Bill of Rights / Elaine Cassel.—   1st ed.
        p. cm.
    Includes bibliographical references.
    ISBN 1-55652-555-9
    1. Civil rights—United States.   2. National security—Law and
legislation—United States.   3. War on Terrorism, 2001–   4. United
States. Uniting and Strengthening America by Providing Appropriate
Tools Required to Intercept and Obstruct Terrorism (USA PATRIOT
ACT) Act of 2001.   I. Title.
KF4749.C33 2004
342.7308'5—DC22   2004010391

———————————

To the lawyers who fight on the front lines in the war against civil liberties
and the judges who have the courage to defend the Constitution

———————————

Cover design: Joan Sommers Design
Cover photo: © AFP/CORBIS
Interior design: Monica Baziuk

First edition
Published by Lawrence Hill Books
An imprint of Chicago Review Press, Incorporated
814 North Franklin Street
Chicago, Illinois 60610
ISBN 1-55652-555-9
Printed in the United States of America
5   4   3   2   1

CONTENTS

2

THE WAR in the COURTS—33

3

THE WAR AGAINST LAWYERS—71

4

GUILT by ASSOCIATION The Islamic Charities—87

5

SEIZURES, DETENTIONS, and DEPORTATIONS—107

6

POPULAR RESISTANCE in the WAR on CIVIL LIBERTIES—131

7

A WAR WITHOUT END—145

ACKNOWLEDGMENTS

THIS BOOK BEGAN with an article I wrote in April 2003 for the Minneapolis, Minnesota, *City Pages* entitled "The Other War: The War at Home." Steve Perry, *City Pages'* editor, asked me to write about the Patriot Act in a way that would appeal to the lay reader. As a student, teacher, and practitioner of the law living in the suburbs of Washington, D.C., where much of the action was unfolding in this new "war," I was absorbed by how quickly life and the law were changing in response to the attacks of September 11, 2001. My experience in the law had taught me that the machinery of new legislation grinds methodically, at best, and slowly, at worst. Rarely do new ideas become laws quickly. And by the time a law is passed, it has usually gone through the many changes and iterations necessary to please competing interests and political parties. Yet the Patriot Act and, to a slightly lesser extent, the Homeland Security Act of 2002, were enacted with alacrity; meaningful debate was abandoned as lawmakers rushed to legislate ways of preventing future attacks on our country. Several of the federal government's prosecution of cases related to its war on terrorism took place in my backyard, in federal court in Alexandria, Virginia. I knew the judges and many of the attorneys who were involved, and, as such, my interest in the subject was both academic and personal.

Positive feedback about "The Other War" led Perry to offer me a Web site hosted by *City Pages* and devoted to civil liberties. Thus, Civil Liberties Watch (http://babelogue.citypages.com:8080/ ecassel/) became a diary of my observations of the "other" war. Articles I've written on the topic have also appeared online in *Findlaw's Writ* and *CounterPunch*. Yuval Taylor, editor at Lawrence Hill Books, read "The Other War" and asked me to develop the topic and write a book. I then began to focus on how to organize my observations in a way that would appeal to a varied audience. The more I learned, the more I felt compelled to share the story of how, in my view, the government was using the war on terrorism to circumvent precious liberties and rights guaranteed by the Bill of Rights. In telling this story, I have tried to place discrete and disparate events into a larger context.

I am grateful to those who have supported my effort. Astute readers sent me stories or leads that found their way into the manuscript. Steve Perry and the staff at *City Pages* supported my Web site editorially and technically. Interviews by foreign media reporters in Germany, Turkey, and Australia helped to sharpen my focus on how events at home were perceived by citizens in other parts of the world. At times, it seemed that the concern of the foreign press was far greater than that of our own. Their interest both delighted and depressed me.

In addition to my own voracious reading, which some days was overwhelming (and by that I mean there was both too much reading and too much bad news), several individuals shared information and helped me think through the themes presented in this book. My editor at *CounterPunch*, Jeffrey St. Clair, was a constant supporter of my writing and a provider of updates on events and incidents about which I would not have otherwise known. Bruce Jackson (SUNY Distinguished Professor and Samuel P. Capen Professor of American Culture, State University of New York at Buffalo) critiqued my writing, provided information from primary sources, and listened patiently to my musing and theorizing. Attorneys who were deeply involved in many of these cases, particularly Michael Tigar and Ashraf Nubani, generously gave their time to help me understand the subtleties of some of the cases that were far more—and far less—than the news reports indicated. Georgetown University Law Professor David Cole, author of two books on topics central to this work—*Terrorism and the Constitution* and *Enemy Aliens*—was a valuable source of information and inspiration. I thank him for taking the time to meet with me and share information about his involvement in legal challenges arising out of the war at home.

My deepest appreciation goes to my editors at Lawrence Hill Books. While Yuval Taylor worked with me in the early stages to shape my unwieldy ideas into a coherent whole, Lisa Rosenthal was there when it mattered the most—when the joy of writing faded into the tedium of producing as well-written and accurate a book as time and resources would permit. Lisa's deft skills as an editor were instrumental; she asked probing questions and smoothed out the rough edges. However, her ever-cheerful responses to my cranky e-mails and her offers to pitch in and help with onerous tasks outside the scope of her duties are what really saw me through. My copy editor, Laura Hensley, also aided the process immeasurably. Her careful reading, fact-checking, and correcting made the book as good as it could be, given my limited abilities as a writer. As all authors will likely agree, any errors and inadequacies in the book are my own. My editors were flawless in their professionalism and support.

My family and friends supported me by allowing me to regale them with a steady stream of bad news and encouraging me to occasionally leave the computer and the newspapers to enjoy the good things that life—and life in America—still offers. They challenged me to counter my criticism of events at home and abroad with the recognition that I still have the freedom to read and talk about what troubles me, while gently suggesting that something other than the Patriot Act might occasionally be a fine topic for family and social gatherings.

The impetus to care so deeply about the future of this country comes from my greatest inspirations, my two grandchildren, Kristin and Matthew. I trust that they and their children will enjoy the benefits of freedom from government intrusion and over-reaching that are supposed to be protected by the Bill of Rights. Such will not be the case if we sit by and watch our freedoms dissolve under the guise of fighting terrorism.

INTRODUCTION

The terrorist attacks of September 11, 2001, were acts of war against the United States of America, its allies, friends, and against the very idea of civilized society. No cause justifies terrorism. The world must respond and fight this evil that is intent on threatening and destroying our basic freedoms and our way of life. Freedom and fear are at war. The enemy is not one person. It is not a single political regime. Certainly it is not a religion. The enemy is terrorism.

> —THE NATIONAL STRATEGY FOR COMBATING TERRORISM,
> *February 4, 2003* [1]

Each action taken by the Department of Justice, as well as the war crimes commissions considered by the President and the Department of Defense, is carefully drawn to target a narrow class of individuals—terrorists. Our legal powers are targeted at terrorists. Our investigation is focused on terrorists. Our prevention strategy targets the terrorist threat.

> —*Remarks of* ATTORNEY GENERAL JOHN ASHCROFT *to Senate Judiciary Committee, December 6, 2001* [2]

Terrorism is a technique. It is not an ideology or a political philosophy, let alone an enemy state. Our leaders' failure to understand that point emerged immediately after Sept. 11, 2001, when they reacted to the attacks in New York and Washington by confusing the hunt for the perpetrators with the Afghan "state" that allegedly "harbored" them. . . . The slippery slope that began with Afghanistan quickly led to the invasion of Iraq, a symbolic and political enormity whose psychological impact Bush and Blair have not yet grasped.

—JONATHAN STEELE, Guardian (London), *November 23, 2003*

How has your life changed since September 11, 2001? Some of you may have witnessed the attacks or lost family members or friends while most of us, thankfully, have been more inconvenienced than actually traumatized. As an example, who among us has not experienced the inconvenience of greater security measures? If you have flown on an airplane, you have stories to tell about lines, delays, and fears about safety. If you work in the health, safety, postal, or law enforcement areas, then everything about the way you do your work has been affected—from working overtime to worrying about anthrax spores floating in the air.

But beyond these overt and rather obvious changes, there are more subtle signs of freedoms lost since September 11. Have you or your car been searched at the airport? Do you have to show a picture identification card to finalize a real estate purchase or to deposit money into your own bank account? Are you worried that your librarian or your Internet service provider may provide information about you to the Federal Bureau of Investigation (FBI) or the Department of Justice? Have you been to a federal court lately and found it harder to get into than Fort Knox?

Now, secret lists govern whether you can get on an airplane, open a bank account, or buy a house; there is secret surveillance of e-mail and the Internet; and new laws allow the government to search your home, your bank records, and your medical files without your knowledge of the search itself or of the information obtained. And that's not all. For example, in 2002, when the FBI wondered if scuba divers might plant explosives in boats, it asked for and received, just for the asking, the names and addresses of more than ten million certified American scuba divers.

Life in America changed in dozens of ways after September 11. Whether by necessity or out of hysterical overreaction, most of the changes mentioned above will be with us for a long time into the future—perhaps forever. For most Americans, this is mostly a nuisance: inconvenience in travel, tightened security at work. But for some Americans and non-Americans living in this country, life has changed in far more serious ways, ways that deprive them of freedom and put them at risk of being at the wrong end of the prosecutorial and deportation powers of the United States. Immigrants nationwide have been jailed indefinitely over visa violations that in the past would have been ignored, and about 13,000 face deportation. Many deportation hearings are conducted in secret, with the use of secret evidence—a change in the law authorized after September 11. The government has locked up dozens of American citizens as "material witnesses" to nebulous grand jury proceedings. In November 2003 a federal appeals court ruled that people who have been charged with no crime and who are suspected of no wrongdoing whatsoever can be jailed in order to give testimony, and their detentions can continue indefinitely. Some have been held for a year or longer and have no hope of seeing the light of day. Two Americans have been interned in military prisons. They have been charged with no crime, and for almost two years they had no access to attorneys or the courts. Federal prosecutors have extracted guilty pleas—to charges such as supporting an unpopular political cause—from dozens of people they threatened with serious terrorism charges, life in prison, or removal to a military prison if they did not confess to charges and cooperate with government investigations.

There is no doubt that Americans have suffered monumental losses of liberty since September 11. It has taken a while for the consequences to be understood, since the laws that brought the biggest changes—the USA Patriot Act and the Homeland Security Act—passed almost stealthlike through a Congress in which many members did not read the laws (as some admit) or were prepared to give up our freedoms in the name of national security. While courts uphold the incursions on freedom, the frustration and fear of the general population are evident in the 200-and-counting municipalities that have denounced the Patriot Act and urged their local law-enforcement officers not to assist the federal government in spying on them.

With all the powers given to the government to fight "terror," President George W. Bush and Attorney General John Ashcroft say they need more—many more. And they are getting them, either through new laws tacked onto unrelated bills in Congress or through executive orders. For instance, in November 2003 Ashcroft signed an executive order that allows FBI agents to hand over surveillance data to local police and ask these local police to aid them in watching "suspicious" individuals. This will likely lead to arrests of "suspicious" persons for minor infractions (for example, an expired vehicle registration or an unpaid parking ticket) in order to get them into custody. These types of pretextual arrests have been used on thousands of immigrants, many of whom have been arrested and deported for minor legal infractions that took place ten, even twenty years in the past.

Consider these three examples, reported in the *Sacramento Bee*, which represent only a few of the thousands of stories reported in the media since September 11:

❖ Two middle-aged peace activists from San Francisco find themselves singled out by authorities in August 2002 as they try to board a flight to Boston for a family visit. Jan Adams and Rebecca Gordon are held and questioned for hours before being released at San Francisco International Airport because their names apparently popped up on a secret government "no fly" list. Both are suing the federal government, with the help of the American Civil Liberties Union (ACLU), in a bid to gain more information about such lists.

❖ After someone apparently overhears a political debate in which he suggests that "Bush is out of control," a forty-year-old public defender surfing the Web on a library computer in Santa Fe, New Mexico, finds himself surrounded by four local police officers and then handcuffed and detained by Secret Service agents. Andrew O'Connor's experience in February 2003, during which he was questioned about whether he was a threat to the president, led to legislative hearings in New Mexico on the Patriot Act and government secrecy.

❖ In October 2001 Barry Reingold, a sixty-two-year-old retired phone company worker, gets into an intense debate at his San Francisco gym over the bombing of Afghanistan and his criticism of President Bush. He is awakened at his Oakland apartment a week later by two FBI agents who want to talk to him about his political beliefs.[3]

On September 15, 2001, President Bush declared a "war" on "terror." It will be, he said, "a conflict without battlefields or beachheads."[4] Actually, there have been battlefields and beachheads—first in Afghanistan in 2001, then in Iraq in 2003. But within a few weeks of the September 11 attacks, another war was declared. It was a war on civil liberties that was fought, ostensibly, to aid the war on terror. In order to win this ideological war with unconventional soldiers, the Bush administration, led by Attorney General Ashcroft, set out to change laws so as to meet what it said were exigent demands—for this war, which, in Bush's words, "will not be short."[5]

Actually, the Bush administration had already given indications—long before September 11—that it would be no friend to
civil liberties. It placed restrictions on the Freedom of Information
Act (the law that allows citizens to access information about how
their government operates), continued to call for draconian prison
terms for drug addicts in the name of the wars on crime and drugs,
and pushed for a law that restricts federal judges' ability to fashion
appropriate sentences for criminals.

Since September 11, other disturbing actions centered on free
speech. Bush's Secret Service agents enforce a "protest-free zone"
around the president so that he is not exposed to the placards or
shouts of Americans who disagree with him. In fact, the Secret Service also enforced this zone when the president visited Great
Britain and Australia in 2003. A man who violated the Secret Service's demand that he remove his antiwar sign is being prosecuted
in Columbia, South Carolina. The FBI has admitted that it is conducting surveillance of antiwar rallies and protestors.

The focus of this book is the Bush administration's curtailment
of civil liberties and how this policy is directly tied to the war on
terrorism. Like the war on terrorism, this war was undertaken in
the name of national security and in defense of "freedom." The
individual victims are diverse: citizens, noncitizens, legal aliens,
and illegal aliens. Institutional victims include Muslim charities,
organizations that support Palestinians, and activist mosques. The
rule of law and the Constitution are also victims. It can no longer
be said that we have three strong, independent branches of government: the executive, the legislative, and the judicial. This country's founders, about whom much is written these days, planned
these three coequal branches precisely to deter the power of a
despotic president. But rather than protect us from an overzealous
executive branch, Congress and the courts are providing Bush with
important ammunition. Hundreds of new laws and regulations have
been enacted, hundreds of old laws have been amended, and the

most massive government reorganization since the New Deal has been put into place—all in the name of fighting "terrorism." Many federal judges, including 171 Bush appointees who were picked because of their loyalty to the president and their tendency to side with him in legal battles, stand ready to thwart efforts to curtail the administration's slashing of civil liberties.

It is important to focus on the liberties sacrificed in the name of this war on terrorism for several reasons. The administration has done a great public relations job selling its belief that some freedoms must be sacrificed in the name of national security. From the day the war on terrorism was declared, Ashcroft has been labeling those who criticize his tactics as being soft on terrorism. The ultimate branding coup came when some government staffer dreamed up the acronym USA PATRIOT (Uniting and Strengthening America by Providing Appropriate Tools Required to Intercept and Obstruct Terrorism) Act for a law that makes a mockery of constitutional protections. The title of the law suggests that to be against the Patriot Act makes one, well, *unpatriotic.* Finally, some aspects of the war on civil liberties harken back to World War II, when fear and claims of national protection led to the internment of Japanese American citizens. The rounding up of thousands of immigrants immediately after September 11 and the lengthy imprisonment of hundreds of them recall a dark chapter in our country's history, a chapter that, it is important to remember, was held to be perfectly legal by the U.S. Supreme Court.

Americans can count on no one in their government to protect them from this loss of liberty. Valiant organizations such as the American Civil Liberties Union (ACLU) and the Center for Constitutional Rights (CCR) have instituted hundreds of lawsuits all over the country, but whatever victories are won in lower federal courts are often either lost on appeal or negated by contrary rulings in other federal circuits. The Supreme Court has, at the time this book went to press, yet to decide the legal challenges to the new powers of the government (though several are pending); when it does hear the cases, the bets are in favor of the president. Supreme Court justices Sandra Day O'Connor and Ruth Bader Ginsburg, virtual ideological opposites on the court, have joined moderate Justice Anthony Kennedy in making public statements that Americans may have to give up some liberties in order to secure freedom for ourselves, our children, and their children. Presciently, prior to September 11, Chief Justice William Rehnquist wrote a book about the powers of the president in a time of "war"—and those powers are virtually without limit or question.

The "war" on "terrorism" is a war that can, by its very terms, never end. It is and will continue to be fought all over the globe. Afghanistan and Iraq are likely only the first of many fronts. To be sure, we may not engage in war in other countries as we have in Afghanistan and Iraq, but President Bush may have Iran, Syria, and Cuba, so-called state sponsors of terrorism, in his sights. But the war on civil liberties is fought at home. In this war, individuals are the secondary casualties. The primary casualties are the freedoms that, according to President Bush, provided the motive for the September 11 attacks. As this book goes to press, the war is continuing unabated, the casualties are mounting, and victory is nowhere in sight. Future generations will either look back and decide that it was "worth it," or they will wonder where we were and what we were doing when the America as we knew it changed.

In the following pages we look at the fronts upon which the war at home is being fought. Chapter 1 examines the laws that support the war. Chapter 2 examines the role of the courts in exercising (or not exercising) oversight of illegal actions of the government, as well as some of the more significant legal battles. Chapter 3 looks at the role of attorneys as combatants and casualties. Chapter 4 examines the guilt-by-association method of prosecution that led to the wholesale shutdown of Muslim charities. Chapter 5 looks at the deplorable plight of thousand of immigrants, who bear the most casualties in this war. Chapter 6 examines the growing local resistance movement. Chapter 7 considers the immediate and long-term implications of these continuing wars—the war on terror and the war on civil liberties. The afterword is an effort to update the reader on events that transpired between the time the manuscript was finalized and when the book went to press.

The late civil rights attorney and activist William Kunstler, who if he were alive today would surely be fighting with the ACLU and the CCR as he did during his long and distinguished career, delivered, as his last public speech, the 1995 commencement address at the School of Architecture at the State University of New York at Buffalo. Speaking on his favorite topic, the Bill of Rights, he said:

> We've come to the point, I guess, where we fear so much—crime in the streets, bombings, domestic terrorism, and the like—that we are virtually willing to countenance giving up of rights because we think it will safeguard us in our daily lives, particularly in the urban centers of this country. We are succumbing, in a way, and I don't make the analogy too close, to what the German people did when the Third Reich began to plant its foot on human rights in Germany. It was better to have a strong man; it was better to curtail rights, to be safe from the Bolsheviks, to be safe from the Versailles Treaty, and so on. And they gave in to that fear, and fear is the most dangerous quotient in any community, democratic or otherwise. Once fear takes root, then people will say, "What does it matter really if he didn't get his Fifth, or Fourth, or Sixth or Eighth Amendment rights? That doesn't affect me. I'm not on trial for anything; I'm not in jail. What does it matter?" That's the question Pastor Niemoller faced, when he said, "They first came for the Jews and I did not raise my voice, and then they came for me." [6]

Substitute *foreign terrorism* for the ills that were so feared in 1995, and you have a pretty fair statement of what is going on in the United States today. But Kunstler was no pessimist. He called on the students to continue to fight for the freedoms that literally define this country.

This book points out what has been lost in less than three years; but the loss need not be permanent. The war against civil liberties need not be won by the government. We, the people, will have the final say—either by saying and doing much or by saying and doing little.

1

TERRORISM, PATRIOTISM, and HOMELAND SECURITY

The Legal Foundation for the War at Home

Our war on terror begins with al Qaeda, but it does not end there. It will not end until every terrorist group of global reach has been found, stopped, and defeated.

—PRESIDENT GEORGE W. BUSH, *September 20, 2001* [1]

When President George W. Bush declared a war on "terror," no one, not even Bush himself, could have envisioned how this war would be carried out. Soon it became clear that there would be a war in Afghanistan that would lead to the deaths not only of America's enemies, but also of Afghani civilians as well as military and civilian personnel from the United States and its allies. But President Bush also put Americans on notice that it would take more than military might to wage this war. The campaign would require a new arsenal of laws and regulations at home. The president got just that. A month after Bush's declaration of war, Attorney General John Ashcroft led a virtually unquestioning Congress to enact laws that would change the concept of what it means to be "free" in America that dated back over 200 years. If the September 11 hijackers hated us for our freedoms, as Bush said, today there is far less to hate.

The legal firepower behind the war on terror consists of three pieces of legislation—the Antiterrorism and Effective Death Penalty Act of 1996, the USA Patriot (Uniting and Strengthening America by Providing Appropriate Tools Required to Intercept and Obstruct Terrorism) Act of 2001, and the Homeland Security Act of 2002—as well as a host of executive orders and federal agency regulations. Ashcroft, Bush, and numerous federal courts have decreed that freedoms must be curtailed in the name of fighting terrorism. But that formulation suggests that this curtailment will be temporary. Given the nature of terrorism—and of politics—that is extremely unlikely. Bush, after all, has said repeatedly that this is to be a war of many years' duration, a life's work. It will not end until every threat the United States identifies as terrorist is vanquished. It is a global war without territorial boundaries and without a known cast of enemies, save one: "evil." And it's being fought at home, in churches and town squares, in courtrooms and libraries.

At the center of this new body of antiterrorism and homeland security laws lies a vague and amorphous definition of its central term: "terrorism." What is "terrorism"? As revealed throughout this book, there are as many definitions as there are laws and regulations using the term. The Patriot Act defines terrorism as "acts dangerous to human life that are a violation of criminal law" that "appear to be intended to influence the policy of a government by intimidation or coercion." This definition is so broad that practically any act of civil disobedience could be construed to be "terrorism." (A political demonstration taking place in the path of an ambulance, for example, could be termed "dangerous to human life.") Under the Patriot Act, any organization that engages in legitimate as well as illegitimate activities can be presumed a terrorist organization for all purposes (see chapter 4). And the prohibited activity that lands a group on the government's list need not consist of violent acts directed at people; anything that is intended to destabilize a government or "influence" its policy by coercion can be termed terrorism. Flooding a congressional office with e-mails critical of government policies and jamming a server in the process—is that an act of terror? Some organizations that use the Internet to ask people to e-mail members of Congress fear that it might be so construed.

As well they should. For the war on terror now encompasses a breathtaking range of new government powers here at home. More than ever before, merely dissenting could make you a target in the Bush administration's war on terror. Indeed, protestors against the war in Iraq and against U.S. trade and monetary policies abroad have discovered that the First Amendment's protections of freedom of speech and assembly can be curtailed at the whim of the executive branch of the government—all in the name of fighting terrorism.

The Bill of Rights

What we think of as *civil liberties*, a term first coined in the mid-seventeenth century, refers to individual rights free from the powers of the government. In the strictest sense, civil liberties are liberties inherent in our bodies, our homes, our minds, our churches, our travel, and our associations. These most elemental of freedoms, along with rights of the people in the face of government power, were granted to Americans in the Bill of Rights. Ironically, these most cherished of American values were not a part of the original Constitution. The Bill of Rights came about primarily through the efforts of George Mason, Virginia's delegate to the Constitutional Convention of 1787. Having crafted a Bill of Rights for the Virginia Constitution, Mason was distressed that the framers of the federal Constitution made no such provision. The Articles of Confederation, he pointed out, were all about federal power, leaving open the opportunity for centralized tyranny—a prospect familiar to the former subjects of King George III.

After Mason left the convention in protest over its failure to adopt provisions that protect individual liberties, the first Congress of the United States adopted twelve amendments to the Constitution on September 25, 1789, and proposed them to the states for ratification. The Constitution required then, as it does now, that the proposed amendments be ratified by three-quarters of the states. Two of the proposed amendments that addressed the number of congressional representatives and their compensation were not ratified. But the other ten were, and on December 15, 1791, they became the first ten amendments to the Constitution—what we know today as the Bill of Rights.

In the name of fighting a war on "terror," the Bush administration, with the help of Congress and the courts, has trampled on the Bill of Rights, particularly the First, Fourth, Fifth, Sixth, and Eighth Amendments, and curtailed many of the freedoms it granted. We will examine far too many instances in subsequent chapters. For example:

❖ The First Amendment protects our right to freely exercise our religion, to freely speak and publish, to peacefully assemble, and to petition our government for a redress of grievances. Of course, none of these rights, nor any other rights given in the Bill of Rights, are without exception. Hundreds of laws and thousands of federal court decisions have shaped them. But under Bush and Ashcroft, Muslims have been preemptively prosecuted for what some say are their religious practices (see chapter 2); people have been investigated and arrested for protesting government policies related to the wars in Iraq and Afghanistan, with some local authorities denying permits for antigovernment protests and, even when permits were granted, arresting peaceful protestors (see afterword); people's reading habits have been subject to scrutiny by the Federal Bureau of Investigation (FBI) and the Department of Justice; and federal agents have infiltrated meetings and conventions of lawyers, law students, and organizations such as the ACLU, as well as gatherings in mosques.

❖ The Fourth Amendment protects us against unreasonable government searches of our homes, businesses, personal effects, and persons, and requires that searches be supported by warrants—issued by judicial officers—that describe the person or thing to be searched. Through the Patriot Act, Congress gave Bush and Ashcroft carte blanche to run roughshod over this amendment. Our computers, phones, and mail as well as business and medical records can be seized by the government without any notice to us, with a simple allegation that it is in the interest of national security to do so.

❖ The Fifth Amendment requires that our life, property, and liberty not be taken away by the government without due process of law. "Due process" generally means being notified of the government's intention of prosecuting or taking our possessions and being given an opportunity to be heard and to protect ourselves and our belongings. Bush and Ashcroft have devised many ways to circumvent this amendment. Muslim charities (see chapter 4) have seen their assets frozen, their offices shuttered, their directors subject to investigation, and their tax returns audited based upon secret evidence that the government refuses to disclose to them. The names of tens of thousands of Americans are on "no fly" lists, lists that subject them to increased security checks at airports. They are not told how their names got on the lists, and there is no mechanism for removing them. People who have been charged with no crime have been imprisoned for months, even a year or more in a few instances, to testify before grand juries or to be interrogated by government agents. The Fifth Amendment's protection against self-incrimination is violated when a statement or confession is coerced by force or threat. At least one American citizen and one Canadian citizen have been imprisoned by foreign countries at our government's request in order to be interrogated (see chapter 5). Some believe that they were sent abroad in order to be tortured into confessing—though the men claim they do not know what crime they are supposed to confess to. Early indications from prisoners recently released from Guantanamo Bay, Cuba, suggest that the military is conducting experiments in psychological interrogation techniques on prisoners, with questioning allowed for up to sixteen hours a day.

❖ The Sixth Amendment protects procedures designed to give defendants a fair trial. Attorney General John Ashcroft, using the power of executive orders to mandate procedures, has wreaked havoc on this amendment's protections. He ordered that trials of certain immigrants be held in secret, contrary to the Sixth Amendment's promise of public trials. Ashcroft also ordered that communications between certain defendants and their attorneys be monitored and recorded on audio- and videotapes, a heretofore unheard-of intrusion on the right to counsel. The right to counsel in a case in which the government is the prosecutor means little if the government can listen in on a defendant's conversations with an attorney. Prosecutors under the jurisdiction of Ashcroft have refused to produce important witnesses in the only two trials that directly involve the September 11 attacks (see chapter 2), jeopardizing the legitimacy of the trials. Ashcroft and his prosecutors undermined the fair trial of an alleged terrorist cell in Detroit, Michigan, leading the sitting judge to publicly rebuke Ashcroft, replace the prosecutors, and consider granting a new trial (see chapter 2).

...ent, as interpreted by statutes and judicial ...hat criminal defendants be granted bail ...nger to the community or are flight risks. ...ms and Arabs who have jobs, families, ties ...d no prior criminal record are facing trials ...nd nonviolent offenses (such as visa fraud ...rtain transactions with foreign countries), ...bail. Part of the government's strong-arm ...et the defendants languish in jail, lose their ...e well-being of their families in the hopes that they will cave in and confess. And many do, as we will see in chapter 2. Not only does this appear to be an unreasonable denial of bail, but it constitutes punishment without conviction. A Department of Justice regulation that allowed federal prosecutors to reverse an immigration-law judge's release of an immigrant on bond pending a deportation trial was recently ruled unconstitutional by a Bush-appointed San Francisco federal judge. A Department of Homeland Security regulation that became effective October 31, 2003, allows government lawyers to override an immigration judge's bond order by filing a form that automatically stays the order until the Board of Immigration Appeals makes a finding. The regulation, which was passed without public comment, does not provide any mandatory time frame for the appeal board to make a custody determination— effectively allowing an individual to be detained indefinitely. A regulation that allows a prosecutor in Ashcroft's employ to override a federal judge is not just unthinkable, it is a gross breach of the principle of the separation of powers. A system in which the prosecutors usurp judges was no doubt an Ashcroft dream come true, that is until the Republican judge sounded the wake-up call.[2]

✧ In addition to bail provisions, the Eighth Amendment prohibits cruel and unusual punishment, a mandate that is commensurate with the maxim "Let the punishment fit the crime." We will discuss cases in which defendants who have not been convicted of any overt act are given long prison sentences, with no possibility of parole since there is no longer parole in the federal system (and has not been for some time). Charged with conspiracy or aiding and abetting terrorism, some are victims of being associated with someone labeled a terrorist or of supporting a cause or organization that is not supported by our government.

Throughout this book, selective cases and incidents illustrative of the most egregious government intrusions into our civil liberties will be examined.

The 1996 Antiterrorism and Effective Death Penalty Act [3]

To all my fellow Americans . . . I say, one thing we owe those who have sacrificed is the duty to purge ourselves of the dark forces which gave rise to this evil. They are forces that threaten our common peace, our freedom, our way of life.

—PRESIDENT BILL CLINTON, April 23, 1995, speaking of the Oklahoma City bombing [4]

Most critics of the war on terrorism's assault on civil liberties mark its beginning with the Clinton administration's Antiterrorism and Effective Death Penalty Act of 1996. But the U.S. government's propensity for spying on its own citizens on the professed grounds of national security goes back much further, and not just as a relic of the days when FBI Director J. Edgar Hoover engaged in illegal surveillance of American citizens. As recently as the 1980s, the FBI conducted surveillance of Americans involved in a variety of causes. Activists who supported rebel groups in El Salvador, attended rallies protesting American aid to the Salvadoran military, signed petitions, or possessed reading material associated with the Committee in Solidarity with the People of El Salvador (CISPES) were targeted for activities labeled as "terrorist" or "leftist." These investigations were conducted for more than two years, until they were finally halted by congressional hearings and the exposure of documents obtained under Freedom of Information Act (FOAI) requests. Congress denounced the scope of the anti-CISPES investigations and in 1994 enacted a law protecting First Amendment activities from FBI investigations.

However, that law was expressly repealed by the 1996 Antiterrorism and Effective Death Penalty Act. This act was the Clinton administration's comprehensive response to both political and personal violent crime. Making the death penalty "effective" meant making it harder to appeal convictions of capital offenses. In terms of fighting terrorism, the law was a reaction to bombings of the World Trade Center in 1993 and the Oklahoma City federal building in 1995. Like the USA Patriot Act, it passed the Senate easily: 91–8. (Bill Clinton also cited the suspicious crash of TWA Flight 800 and the bombing at Atlanta's Olympic Village in 1996 as further proof of the dangers supporting the new legislation.)

The 1996 Antiterrorism and Effective Death Penalty Act provides an eight-year window to see whether or not such acts work as a tool against terrorism. Is there any evidence whatsoever that this act has actually succeeded in stopping any terrorist activity? Not according to its critics. The law never yielded any significant protection against terrorism—everything a terrorist does was already illegal—although it did lead to substantial incursions on constitutional rights, such as:

✢ allowing the government to deport immigrants based on undisclosed evidence;

❖ making it a crime to support even the lawful activities of an organization labeled a terrorist group by the State Department;

❖ authorizing the FBI to investigate the crime of "material support" for terrorism (see below) based solely on activities protected under the First Amendment, including specifically allowing agents to attend religious services at mosques "under cover";

❖ freezing assets of any U.S. citizen or domestic organization believed to be an agent of a terrorist group, without specifying how an "agent" was identified;

❖ expanding the powers of the secret court that administers the Foreign Intelligence Surveillance Act (FISA), a court in which federal judges sit in secret to consider—and mostly rubber-stamp—Justice Department requests for widespread surveillance of "terrorists";

❖ repealing the law that barred the FBI from opening investigations based solely on activities protected under the First Amendment—such as the anti-CISPES investigations—and allowing such surveillance to go forward if the individuals were believed to be associated with any person or organization labeled "terrorist";

❖ allowing the Immigration and Naturalization Service (now called the United States Citizenship and Immigration Services [USCIS]) to deport citizens (mostly Muslims) upon the order of INS officials. The evidence typically was not disclosed to the deportees, and the decisions of the INS officials were not subject to challenge in a federal court.

As we will see in chapters 2 and 4, many prosecutions have been brought under the provision of the Antiterrorism Act that bars giving "material support" to organizations on the State Department's terrorist list. The section at issue, 18 U.S.C. 2339B, has been a central tool in the Bush administration's criminal "war on terrorism" cases.[5] In 2000 the U.S. Court of Appeals for the Ninth Circuit ruled that the terms "training" and "personnel," as used in the 1996 act, were unconstitutionally vague. The Patriot Act did not redefine these terms, but it amended the language to include "monetary instruments" and "expert advice or assistance." On December 3, 2003, the U.S. Court of Appeals for the Ninth Circuit ruled that this statute was likewise unconstitutionally vague. The Bush administration was interpreting the statute to ensnare even people who had no reason to know that an organization was on a government watch list and who also had no knowledge of any so-called "terrorist" activities of the organization. (See chapter 4 for this ruling.)

The USA Patriot Act of 2001

> How will we fight and win this war? We will direct every resource at our command—every means of diplomacy, every tool of intelligence, every instrument of law enforcement, every financial influence, and every necessary weapon of war—to the disruption and to the defeat of the global terror network.
>
> —PRESIDENT BUSH, September 20, 2001 [6]

Attorney General Ashcroft proposed the laws that became the USA Patriot Act three days after September 11. He deputized a young Department of Justice attorney on leave from Georgetown University Law School, Viet Dinh, to be the principal drafter of the legislation. Dinh, a boat refugee from Vietnam who attended high school in California, approached the task with a missionary-like zeal. He "slept with" the Federalist Papers (a series of eighty-five essays written by John Jay, Alexander Hamilton, and James Madison, which are more concerned with the powers of the government than the rights of the people) during the weeks he was drafting the legislation, spending much of the time sleeping in his office. He welcomed the opportunity to "give back" to his country by writing a law "that would protect freedom by attacking liberty's threats." [7]

WHAT THE USA PATRIOT ACT DOES [8]

The USA Patriot Act gives law enforcement officials broader authority to conduct electronic surveillance and wiretaps and gives the president the authority, when the nation is under actual attack by a foreign entity, to confiscate any property within U.S. jurisdiction of anyone believed to be engaging in such attacks. The measure also tightens oversight of financial activities to prevent money laundering and to diminish bank secrecy, all in an effort to disrupt terrorist finances. The act, almost 400 pages in length, amends dozens of existing laws. It also stretches the Bill of Rights in several respects. It particularly allows incursions into rights protected by the First and Fourth Amendments.[9] Some of the more controversial civil rights incursions had been on the executive branch's "wish list" for many years.[10] September 11 provided just the impetus needed to change the rules of criminal procedure for all crimes—not just crimes of terror. The more drastic incursions on civil liberties resulting from the Patriot Act include:

❖ It is a crime for anyone in this country to contribute money or other support to the activities of a group on the State Department's terrorist watch list. Organizations are so designated on the basis of secret evidence, and their inclusion on the list cannot be challenged in court (see chapter 4).

❖ The FBI can obtain warrants that "follow" a person across state lines and trace any telephone or computer usage. Prior to the Patriot Act, warrants had to be obtained in each state and for each phone number where a person could be located. Now, one warrant, often obtained in the highly conservative federal court in Alexandria, Virginia, can be enforced wherever the person is found.

❖ The FBI can monitor and tape conversations and meetings between an attorney and a client who is in federal custody, whether the client has been convicted, charged, or merely detained as a material witness. New York City attorney Lynne Stewart (the court-appointed representative of Sheik Abdel Rahman, who was convicted in the 1993 World Trade Center bombing) was indicted for aiding and abetting terrorism based on conversations with her client (see chapter 3).

❖ The FBI can order librarians to turn over information about their patrons' reading habits and Internet use. The librarian cannot inform the patron that this information has been provided. Librarians, on the whole, are outraged at their new role; some have taken to posting signs in the library warning patrons not to use the Internet, others to destroying their logs of Internet users. One librarian said to a *Washington Post* reporter, "This law is dangerous . . . I read murder mysteries—does that make me a murderer? I read spy stories—does that mean I'm a spy?" [11]

❖ Law enforcement can gain access to information on citizens by obtaining a secret warrant—known as a "sneak-and-peek warrant"—that gives no advance notice to the person whose home or possessions are to be searched. A standard criminal search warrant gives notice to the owner of the premises to be searched and provides a statement of probable cause for the search (i.e., based on reliable information, there is reason to believe that a certain crime has been committed) before the search is conducted. It is served on the person if the person is at home, or it is left at the premises and the search is done later. These new sneak-and-peek warrants allow law enforcement to search first, whether or not the individual in question is present, and give notice to the individual later.

❖ The government can conduct surveillance on the Internet and e-mail use of American citizens without any notice, upon order to the Internet service providers (ISPs). Providers who move to quash such subpoenas may be charged with obstructing justice.

❖ Immigration authorities may detain immigrants without filing any charges for a "reasonable period of time." Immigration authorities need not account for the names or locations of the detainees, and what constitutes a "reasonable period of time" is not defined. Another highly controversial provision of the act (Section 412) permits the U.S. attorney general to detain alien terrorist suspects for up to seven days if he certifies that he has reasonable grounds to believe that the suspects either are engaged in conduct that threatens the national security of the United States or that they are inadmissible or deportable on grounds of terrorism, espionage, sabotage, or sedition. Within the specified seven days, the attorney general must either initiate removal or criminal proceedings or release the alien. If the alien is held, the determination must be reexamined every six months to confirm that the alien's release would threaten national security or endanger some individual or the general public (see afterword for update).

❖ American colleges and universities with foreign students must report extensive information about these students to immigration authorities, who may in turn revoke student visas for missteps as minor as failure to get an advisor's signature on a form that adds or drops classes. College personnel cannot notify students about the lapse in order to save them from deportation.

To a very large extent, campus police and security personnel have become agents of the immigration authorities.

❖ A warrant to conduct widespread surveillance on any American citizen thought to be associated with terrorist activities can be obtained from a secret panel of judges on the special Foreign Intelligence Surveillance Act (FISA) court, with an affidavit from a Department of Justice official. If arrested as a result of the surveillance (as was the case with Attorney Stewart), the defendant has no right to know the facts supporting the warrant request. Prior to the Patriot Act, a FISA warrant could not be obtained to target an American citizen. It was only to be used to gather foreign counterintelligence. Other provisions in the Patriot Act allow those who conduct surveillance to share information with law enforcement authorities. Thus, law enforcement officers can gain access to information obtained without the usual protections against unreasonable search and seizure.

❖ The FBI can conduct aerial surveillance of individuals and homes without a warrant and can install video cameras in places where lawful demonstrations and protests are held. Facial recognition computer programs are used to identify persons the FBI deems suspicious for political reasons. An ACLU employee in South Carolina is being prosecuted for the federal offense of being in a "restricted area" at the Columbia, South Carolina, airport in October 2002, when President Bush made a political campaign appearance. He was not arrested just for being there, but rather because he was displaying an antiwar placard. The U.S. attorney in Columbia, South Carolina, who brought the charge is the son of the late Senator Strom Thurmond (R-SC).

By far the most alarming aspect of the Patriot Act is the way in which it fosters guilt by association—something most Americans think went out with McCarthyism and J. Edgar Hoover. Today, however, the most tenuous connection of an individual to a "terrorist organization" (as designated by the secretary of state) or "terrorist state" can now lead to serious federal charges.

PASSAGE OF THE USA PATRIOT ACT

On September 19, 2001, the Bush administration submitted its statutory antiterrorism package to congressional leaders.[12] On October 1 a much-expanded version of the legislation was introduced formally into the House. A comparable bill was introduced in the Senate on October 4. Typically, in the course of legislation, House and Senate conferees meet in an effort to resolve differences about the legislation in what is called a "conference committee." Of course, House and Senate office buildings had been temporarily shut down due to the anthrax found in the mail. So, what few negotiations there were took place at House and Senate leadership meetings and at informal meetings and through informal agreements among House and Senate negotiators. There were no hearings scheduled, little debate, and no opportunity for negotiating amendments.

The Republicans and Ashcroft have taken most of the heat for pushing for quick passage, but there is plenty of blame to be shared by the Democrats in the House and Senate. One anecdote comes from Senator Feingold, the only senator to vote against the Patriot Act:

> When the original Ashcroft antiterrorism bill came in [the October 4 version of the USA Patriot Act], they wanted us to pass it two days later. I thought this thing was going to be greatly improved. They did get rid of a couple of provisions, like looking into educational records. But there were still twelve or thirteen very disturbing things, and I thought, OK, we'll take care of this. But then

something happened in the Senate, and I think the Democratic leadership was complicit in this. Suddenly, the bottom fell out. I was told
that a unanimous consent agreement was being offered with no
amendments and no debate. They asked me to give unanimous consent. I refused. The majority leader came to the floor and spoke very
sternly to me, in front of his staff and my staff, saying, you can't do
this, the whole thing will fall apart. I said, what do you mean it'll
fall apart, they want to pass this, too. I said, I refuse to consent. [13]

The push for quick passage of the act left virtually no time for
the discussion of its most controversial measures. The truncated
legislative process avoided necessary debate on how to effectively
improve the nation's ability not only to collect intelligence but also
to efficiently and wisely synthesize collected data into useful information. (In the long run, the absence of debates and hearings may
also deprive the judiciary of reliable legislative history when courts
review the meaning and constitutionality of the act.) [14]

In mid-October, the press and civil liberties groups were start-
ing to get wind of the legislation, but there was no time to derail
the legislation. Less than two weeks after the House passed the
initial version on October 24, 2001, the House passed the final version of the Patriot Act by a vote of 357–66, and the next day the
Senate passed the Patriot Act by a vote of 98–1. President Bush
signed the bill into law on October 26, 2001. [15]

About the only significant compromise between the administration and Congress had to do with the more controversial compo-
nents, some of which were set to "sunset" (i.e., automatically expire)
in 2005. According to legislative experts, sunset provisions in laws
are clues to unease among those who approve the legislation. In
terms of the Patriot Act, the reasoning seems to have been: "So
what if the law is controversial and unprecedented in its surveillance
powers and is a constraint on the civil liberties embodied in the first
ten amendments to the constitution? It will only last four years.

Then we can revisit the issues." The problem with such reasoning is that four years is a long time, and liberties once discarded are rarely resurrected. (Indeed, late in 2003 efforts began to make permanent some of the provisions set to expire in 2005.) Patriot Act provisions with this built-in sunset date include:

+ expansion of the time limit on how long secret FISA warrants issued by the FISA court are valid without a new application;

+ expansion of the purpose of FISA warrants (pre–Patriot Act, FISA warrants could only be obtained for the purpose of gathering foreign intelligence on someone said to be an agent of a foreign government. The Patriot Act expanded the scope of these secret warrants to require only that foreign intelligence be a "significant purpose," not the only purpose);

+ sharing of information between domestic law enforcement officials and the Central Intelligence Agency.

Interestingly, some provisions that represent more of a threat to individual freedoms are not set to expire. These include:

+ requiring ISPs to provide personal information and passwords of subscribers;

+ allowing ISPs to forward e-mail to authorities if the e-mail appears to represent a threat of serious injury or death to another person; and

+ continuing the "sneak-and-peek" warrant provision.

Representatives on both sides of the aisle, though, seemed to be mindful of the potential negative political fallout from curtailing civil liberties indefinitely.

THE USA PATRIOT ACT UNDER FIRE [16]

From the time the legislation was first presented to Congress, the members who balked were chastised and all but referred to as traitors. It is not an overstatement to say that Attorney General Ashcroft charged that anyone who opposed the USA Patriot Act should be blamed for future terrorist attacks. On December 6, 2001, Ashcroft defended his department's use of the Patriot Act to detain hundreds of immigrants and to question thousands more. "To those who scare peace-loving people with phantoms of lost liberty, my message is this: your tactics only aid terrorists for they erode our national unity and diminish our resolve," Ashcroft told the Senate Judiciary Committee. "They give ammunition to America's enemies and pause to America's friends. They encourage people of goodwill to remain silent in the face of evil." [17]

In June 2003 the inspector general of the Justice Department, Glenn A. Fine, issued a report documenting the mistreatment of hundreds of foreigners detained after September 11 in violation of provisions in the Patriot Act (see chapter 5).[18] This report did not paint a pretty picture. Fine uncovered information on lengthy detentions without notice to family members, physical and verbal abuse of some detainees, and deportations of hundreds for minor visa violations. Not one terrorist charge was lodged against any of the detainees. (For more on the inspector general's report and the detainees, see chapter 5.)

Attorney General Ashcroft and FBI director Robert Mueller bristled at the criticism and not only insisted that nothing in the act was illegal but also that they would do it all again. In addition to pronouncing that the Patriot Act "did not go far enough," Ashcroft defended the law in a hearing before the House Judiciary Committee:

> The Patriot Act gave us the tools we needed to integrate our law enforcement and intelligence capabilities to win the war on terror. It allowed the Department of Justice to use the same tools from the

criminal process, the same tools on terrorists that we use to combat mobsters or drug dealers. We use these tools to gather intelligence and to prevent terrorists from unleashing more death and
destruction within our country. We use these tools to connect the
dots. We use these tools to save innocent lives.[19]

Because the Patriot Act had been passed in haste, with virtually
no congressional debate and little commentary in the press, it was
not until 2003 that some members of Congress and certain seg-
ments of the public started to express some misgivings about the
law. The debate seemed to be fueled by the leak of what appeared
to be a law dubbed "Patriot II." It was published by the Center for
Public Integrity on its Web site in February 2003.[20] Immediately,
the Justice Department denied that it was anything other than a
"trial balloon," although to most critics it seemed like a final draft
of legislation. It was apparent that Vice President Dick Cheney had
received copies of the legislation.

The leak of Patriot II touched off a firestorm of criticism in Congress and elsewhere, even from Republican quarters. A few conservatives, notably *New York Times* columnist William Safire, were
outraged by much of it.[21] As the press began to report on Patriot II,
Patriot I came more into focus. As a result, hundreds of municipalities held open debates and forums to discuss Patriot I, leading to
more than 200 local and state resolutions against the act.[22] Some local
law enforcement jurisdictions went on record publicly condemning
the law and promising to refuse to cooperate with its enforcement.

In August 2003 Attorney General Ashcroft set out on a campaign tour of sorts. He was not running for reelection—his position is a cabinet-level presidential appointment. He was running
for one thing—to ensure the reelection, as it were, of the Patriot
Act, by the U.S. Congress.[23] With Patriot II out of the picture and
Patriot I under close scrutiny, Ashcroft took to the road and touted
a new version of Patriot II introduced in the Congress, the VIC-
TORY (Vital Interdictions of Criminal Terrorist Organizations)

Act of 2003, which would expand surveillance powers, make some existing crimes (such as drug trafficking) crimes of terror, and create new terrorism crimes.[24] After several stops on his sixteen-city traveling Patriot show tour, which ended (intentionally, no doubt) on the eve of the second anniversary of the September 11 terrorist attacks, it became clear that Ashcroft was not interested in selling the law to ordinary American citizens. In order to get into one of his presentations you had to be a law enforcement agent or associated with television media. He refused admission to anyone else, including print media. His sermon consisted of defending the law, the substance of which is set out on his own government-sponsored Web site, www.lifeandliberty.com. Ashcroft was preaching to the choir.[25] The essence of his message was again—and continues to be—that anyone who is against any aspect of the Patriot Act, or his proposed extensions, is a terrorist sympathizer.

In late summer 2003, the U.S. House of Representatives voted to deny funding to one of the more controversial portions of the law—the so-called sneak-and-peek provision. The funding ban did not pass the Senate, however, and the omnibus spending bill passed by Congress in January 2004 left intact funding for what many see as a violation of the Fourth Amendment's prohibition against unreasonable searches and seizures. Proponents defend the practice by saying that aggrieved persons may seek judicial redress, but that is a disingenuous representation. People may never know about the search, or not know it for a long time, since law enforcement can delay reporting indefinitely if it is deemed in the interests of "national security." (For more on the most recent congressional challenges to the Patriot Act, see chapter 6.)

BEYOND THE PATRIOT ACT

Much of what the Bush administration is doing in the name of fighting terrorism arises from powers exercised by President Bush that are not dependent on the USA Patriot Act. Most of these restrictions on liberty were not part of the letter of the act; they were shaped by means of rules and regulations adopted in agencies and departments of government with little notice to the public. That's because the Patriot Act granted sweeping new powers to agencies such as the Department of Justice, the FBI, and the USCIS to go their own way in prosecuting the war on terrorism (much as the Homeland Security Act would do for its agencies and departments; see below). James Dempscy, executive director of the Center for Democracy and Technology and coauthor of many books on civil liberties, made an interesting observation. The Patriot Act, he says, gets a lot of blame or praise for things that have nothing to do with it. It has, he suggests, become a kind of lightning rod around which civil libertarians rally.[26] In fact, many of the civil rights abuses we are suffering today stem from use (and abuse) of executive powers legally available to President Bush and Attorney General Ashcroft. With the stroke of a pen, they can create policy that may or may not be consistent with the U.S. Constitution. Examples include:

❖ Accused terrorists labeled "enemy combatants" on the order of President Bush can be tried in military tribunals in the United States or abroad under rules of procedure developed by the Pentagon and the Department of Justice. (Under the international laws of war, captured enemies are either lawful or unlawful combatants. Lawful combatants are soldiers who wear the uniform of another country and who fight according to the laws of war. Unlawful, or enemy, combatants are people who claim allegiance to no country but, perhaps, to a cause. The term "enemy combatants" appears nowhere in U.S. criminal law, international law, or in the law of war.) In the Bush Administration, all it takes to be named an enemy combatant is the affidavit of a Pentagon employee, who is not required to provide the rationale for his or her decision, even to a federal judge. In the case of Yaser Hamdi, the federal appellate court ruled that it has no authority to look behind this affidavit and question the determination (see chapter 2). Enemy combatants are also denied counsel and contact with family members. In fact, hundreds of enemy combatants are still being held in Guantanamo Bay, Cuba, without attorneys, without family contact, and under conditions said by some to be tantamount to physical and psychological torture (see chapters 3 and 5).

❖ The Patriot Act cannot be blamed for American citizens being held in military prisons without charges, without lawyers, and without any hope of judicial review. As I'll discuss in chapters 2 and 3, the cases, of "enemy combatants" Hamdi and Jose Padilla (the American Muslim fingered by Ashcroft as a would-be "dirty bomb" builder) arise solely because President Bush has taken that power upon himself, with no law to support it.

❖ The Patriot Act cannot be blamed for the abuse of the "material witness" law, a 1984 statute that allows the government to detain persons at will for an arbitrary period of time to give testimony that might be useful in the prosecutions of others. The law is an exception to the traditional principle that people can generally not be detained in jail unless they are charged with a crime. The law recognizes an exception in certain instances when a witness to a crime needs to be "detained" in order to secure his or her testimony at a hearing or a trial. But the Bush administration has stretched the law to justify locking up people for two years or more in order to provide information about undisclosed "investigations" at some future, but yet-to-be specified date. Padilla was detained as a material witness, and we will discuss the twists and turns of his case in chapter 2.

In these three areas, the Bush administration has created what Dempsey refers to as a "law-free zone," in which, he argues, U.S. laws, international laws, and treaties do not govern the government's behavior and in which the government is free from the constraints of judicial review.[27] The U.S. Congress could enact laws to thwart this executive expansion of lawlessness, but it has shown not the slightest inclination to do so.

The following are examples of infringements on civil liberties not directly attributable to the Patriot Act, but made possible by various regulations and executive orders handed down by law enforcement and immigration authorities:

❖ Aliens and U.S. citizens may be detained and denied access to an attorney without being charged with a crime. The treatment of Padilla is a case in point (see chapter 2).

❖ Resident alien men primarily from Middle Eastern and Muslim countries were required, until late 2003 when the program was abandoned, to report to immigration offices for registration. Hundreds who reported were detained, arrested, tried, and deported for minor immigration infractions. Many were refused the right to appear with an attorney, a refusal that is a violation of U.S. Citizenship and Immigration Services (USCIS, formerly known as the INS) regulations. Though the government has the right, if it chooses, to exercise a zero-tolerance policy for immigration violations, in this instance the policy was enforced only against Arabs and Muslims. (In late 2003 the USCIS announced that it was abandoning this reporting requirement, but it did not say why it was doing so.)

❖ Lawful foreign visitors may be photographed and fingerprinted when they enter the country and may be required to periodically report for questioning. This provision began to be enforced in early 2004.

❖ The Transportation Security Administration (TSA) can search any car at any airport without providing proof of any suspicion of criminal activity.

❖ The TSA can conduct full searches of people boarding airplanes, and if the passenger is a child, the child may be separated
from a parent during the search. An objection by a parent or
guardian to the search will put the objector at risk of being
charged with obstructing a federal law enforcement officer and
being tried in federal court. Travelers in Portland, Oregon, and
Baltimore, Maryland, have reported such arrests.

❖ The TSA is heading up a program to amass all available computerized information on all purchasers of airline tickets in
order to categorize individuals according to their threat to
national security and embed the label on all boarding passes.
The Computer-Assisted Passenger Prescreening System is
designed to perform background checks on all airline passengers and assign each passenger a "threat level." Passengers will
not be able to ascertain their classification or the basis for the
classification. Based on the coding, airline employees and security agents will subject certain passengers to greater pre-board-
ing scrutiny and deny boarding to others.

❖ The TSA distributes a "no fly" list to airport security personnel and airlines that permits refusal of boarding and detention
of persons deemed to present risks of terrorism or air piracy or
who pose a threat to airline or passenger safety. This is an expansion of a regulation that since 1990 has looked out for threats to
civil aviation. Names are added daily based on secret criteria.

HAS THE USA PATRIOT ACT DONE ANY GOOD?

Ashcroft has suggested that not only is America safer because of the
USA Patriot Act, but also that if the law had been in effect on September 11, terrorist attacks would not have occurred. There is simply no evidence for this. If we are any safer than we were on
September 11, 2001, it is the result of improved intelligence about

al Qaeda and other terrorists groups' plans for possible future attacks, such as what led to the government's cancellation of certain Air France and British Airways flights in late December 2003. There is no indication that snooping on American's library and Internet usage, monitoring antiwar protestors, detaining immigrants, or forcing foreign visitors to register have done anything to mitigate against future terror attacks. Not one arrest has resulted from these controversial measures.

In a televised exchange with Bryant Gumbel in August 2003, Viet Dinh and David Cole argued for and against the merits of the Patriot Act. Dinh repeated the party line—that the entire focus of the law was to protect liberty. "Security in the name of liberty" was the catch phrase. Dinh said, "I stressed to [my staff] that security in [and] of itself could not be and in a democratic society should not be an end in [and] of itself but rather it exists only for the ultimate goal of liberty. And so liberty concerns were not concerns as such—they were the ultimate goal of what we were trying to do." [28]

Dinh's glibness belied the fact that there was a tension between security and liberty. But did there need to be? The safety concerns brought about by September 11 were not caused by civil liberties. They were caused by intelligence failures (two of the nineteen hijackers were on a terrorist watch list, yet they boarded the planes using their own names), flawed immigration practices (several were in the United States on expired or illegitimate visas), and lapsed security measures (the hijackers boarded the planes with weapons, breaching airline security requirements). In actuality, the government did not use the means at its disposal to thwart the attacks, nor did it attempt to protect the "homeland" with any less stringent measures than the draconian encroachments of constitutional protections.

In terms of implementation of the Patriot Act, we know that of five thousand foreign nationals detained after September 11, not one was charged with an act terrorism.[29] We know that the act made huge incursions into the First, Fourth, Fifth, Sixth, and Eighth

Amendments of the United States and led to numerous executive orders that further breached established liberties. Congress—and, indirectly, the American people—were asked to give the government increased surveillance and law enforcement powers, insisting that to oppose the act was to invite another terrorist attack. Based on the results of an Associated Press poll released on September 10, 2003, the majority of Americans polled (58 percent of 1,008 respondents) did not believe that the law curtailed their freedoms, but two-thirds believed that the act might do so in the future. Most who agreed that they had lost some liberties felt that the restrictions were enacted to "protect us." [30] This response itself is an ominous warning—a majority of Americans feel that it is acceptable to lose freedom in the name of national security.

On the eve of the second anniversary of the September 11 attacks, President Bush visited the FBI Academy in Quantico, Virginia, and pronounced that the United States needed more Patriot Act–like laws. The gist of his remarks was that we don't have enough tools to fight terror. Police need to be able to go after terrorists like they go after criminals. Acts that are not crimes ought to be crimes of terrorism. Crimes of terror that are not punishable by death must have the death penalty available for prosecution. [31] Bush repeated a call for more laws to fight terror in his January 2004 State of the Union address.

But there is a flaw in Bush's proposals. Terrorist acts, which in the strictest definition are acts that target civilians with violence in order to achieve a political objective, are criminal acts. Criminal laws and procedures are in place to prevent and prosecute such crimes. Those laws have built-in constitutional safeguards, such as the requirement that law enforcement officials must establish criminal intent in order to obtain search warrants and wiretaps and must establish probable cause in order to arrest people. Further, the ability to target al Qaeda or other terrorist groups through counterintelligence has long been made possible through the FISA procedures, in which surveillance wiretaps are readily available upon establishing proof of a foreign national's threat to national security. The history of the FISA court indicates that such requests for warrants were rarely, if ever, denied by the judges who sit in secret on that court. Not content with the mechanisms in place, Bush used the anniversary of September 11 to set the stage for introducing bills that would further extend government power over citizens and non-citizens, in the United States, Iraq, and the next "front" of the war on terror—wherever the president decides that may be.

The Homeland Security Act of 2002 [32]

> With the help of many nations, with the help of 90 nations, we're tracking terrorist activity, we're freezing terrorist finances, we're disrupting terrorist plots, we're shutting down terrorist camps, we're on the hunt one person at a time. Many terrorists are now being interrogated. Many terrorists have been killed. We've liberated a country. We recognize our greatest security is found in the relentless pursuit of these cold-blooded killers. Yet, because terrorists are targeting America, the front of the new war is here in America. Our life changed and changed in dramatic fashion on September the 11th, 2001. . . . The Homeland Security Act of 2002 takes the next critical steps in defending our country. The continuing threat of terrorism, the threat of mass murder on our own soil will be met with a unified, effective response.
>
> —PRESIDENT BUSH, November 25, 2002, upon signing the Homeland Security Act of 2002 into law [33]

After initially rejecting Democratic proposals that there be a unified government agency to coordinate the defense of our borders and the domestic war on terrorism, the Bush administration realized this would be a great political move. It has turned out to be another huge power grab, which has received even less attention than the USA Patriot Act. The salient provisions of the law that created the Department of Homeland Security and further laid the foundation for hundreds of new regulations governing American citizens and businesses are buried in pages of bureaucratic reorganization jargon. Many of the provisions have nothing to do with homeland security, but came out of intensive bargaining for pork barrel projects and protection of agency turfs. As with the Patriot Act, few lawmakers actually read the 484-page document that makes up the Homeland Security Act. The Bush administration succeeded in convincing Congress that there was no time for debate.[34]

Effective on January 1, 2003, the Homeland Security Act created the Department of Homeland Security as a cabinet-level agency; consolidated and moved agency functions (for instance, moving the authority for issuing and denying visas from immigration authorities to the new department); empowered the new department with administrative powers over border protection, transportation, public health, chemical and biological counterterrorism measures, and information collection and dissemination; and gave it broad intelligence-gathering and -sharing functions. As with any law, the statute is only a framework. The devil is in the details—the host of regulations enacted by agencies pursuant to powers granted in the law. For instance, on October 1, 2003, every bank and financial institution in the United States had to comply with strict restrictions designed to monitor possible terrorist money laundering (see chapter 7).

For civil libertarians, the most disturbing provision of the Homeland Security Act is its grant to this department and to the agencies and organizations over which it has regulatory powers many of the same surveillance powers granted to the FBI and the Department of Justice under the Patriot Act. All of the following can take place without judicial oversight or establishing probable cause that a crime is being committed:

❖ The secretary of Homeland Security has access to information from any federal agency, including unevaluated intelligence and electronic databases.

❖ ISPs have the right to voluntarily turn over to a federal, state, or local government entity the contents of e-mail communications if the provider believes that an emergency requires disclosure. Government agents may then use content in the e-mail messages as a pretext for conducting secret surveillance.

❖ Information acquired through any surveillance may be shared with any federal, state, or local governmental agency as long as it is related to national security.

❖ The act severely curtails public access to agency information on any infrastructure (transportation or computer systems, to name only two) the secretary of Homeland Security designates as "critical." Thus, any information about such an infrastructure (e.g., a power plant) can be exempt from an FOIA request. Anyone who releases information about a "critical" infrastructure faces criminal prosecution. This provision has been used to deny public access to information about U.S. Army Corps of Engineers projects.

❖ The secretary of Homeland Security has broad powers to require that a select group of people or the entire population without any exception receives vaccinations if the secretary deems that a "public health emergency" makes such action "advisable." Arguably, a hypothetical threat would be sufficient.

There is no standard for how the secretary could make such a determination because it is purely within his discretion.

✣ Manufacturers of vaccines are exempt from being sued for death or injury caused by the vaccine as long as the drug is licensed by the department, even if the manufacturer is negligent.

✣ The secretary of Homeland Security may form advisory committees and keep the makeup and the conduct of meetings secret.

✣ Broad protections are given to government contractors and vendors of products, supplies, and the like that are part of the "critical infrastructure." Under a provision of the act called the SAFETY (Support Anti-Terrorism by Fostering Effective Technologies) Act, manufacturers and sellers can ask for and obtain blanket protection from public tort claims for injury caused by the products. These products could be anything from assault weapons to burglar alarms, and the protections extend to all uses of the products, not just government uses.[35]

✣ Government contractors who disclose any vulnerabilities in the government's "critical infrastructure" are subject to criminal prosecution. There is no whistle-blower protection for employees in the Department of Homeland Security.

✣ The department can contract with corporations that have organized offshore in order to avoid paying U.S. taxes.

A few of the more draconian surveillance provisions of the Homeland Security Act were denied funding once details were disclosed by the media. But agencies within the Department of Homeland Security are responsible for administering hundreds of regulations that curtail civil liberties, particularly those of travelers and resident aliens (see above).

The full extent of the erosion of liberty occasioned by the passage of the Homeland Security and Patriot acts will not be known or felt for years hence. The words of Senator Feingold remind us why these new laws are so troubling:

> There is no doubt . . . that if we lived in a police state, it would be easier to catch terrorists. If we lived in a country where police were allowed to search your home at any time for any reason; if we lived in a country where the government was entitled to open your mail, eavesdrop on your phone conversations, or intercept your e-mail communications . . . the government would probably discover and arrest more terrorists, or would-be terrorists. . . . But that would not be a country in which we would want to live.[36]

With Congress effectively handing over the reins of power to the executive branch and providing all the tools the Bush Administration wants ostensibly to fight the war on terror, it's up to the federal courts to run interference for the people and to save the Constitution and the rule of law from the Bush administration's campaign to destroy it. Due to Bush's judicial appointments and those of his father, George H. W. Bush, and President Ronald Reagan, conservative Republican judges now make up half of the federal judiciary. We will look at how the federal courts have supported the Bush Administration's war on civil liberties in chapter 2.

2

THE WAR in the COURTS

The Department of Justice has charged over 260 individuals uncovered in the course of terrorist investigations, and convicted or secured guilty pleas from over 140 individuals. The U.S. government has disrupted alleged terrorist cells in Buffalo, Seattle, Portland, Detroit, North Carolina and Tampa.

—WHITE HOUSE PROGRESS REPORT *on the Global War on Terrorism, September 2003* [1]

Shortly after September 11, 2001, the Bush administration began the search for the people who were responsible for the attacks. The results to date have not been promising. At the time this book went to press, not one person directly involved in the attacks had been brought to trial. There have been prosecutions of people who the administration says were or are supporting so-called terrorists. Yet the value of those prosecutions in deterring terrorism is unknown. Indeed, it may be unknowable. What is known is how the prosecutions skirt the law and the Constitution in the name of protecting national security. The Bush administration believes that terrorism prosecutions must be different from criminal prosecutions. It insists that the laws and rules of court that apply to criminal cases—and that exist to protect individuals against the awesome power of the government—should be altered when defendants are terrorists. Many of the cases we will consider have yet to be finally resolved at the time this book went to press. But their histories to date show federal prosecutors trampling on individual rights in the name of preserving "liberty."

The Moussaoui Case

On September 10, 2003, federal prosecutors in Alexandria, Virginia, defied, for a second time, the order of Judge Leonie Brinkema to allow alleged terrorist Zacarias Moussaoui, formerly called the "twentieth" hijacker who did not make it onto one of the September 11 airplanes, access to government witnesses.[2] Under the Federal Rules of Criminal Procedure, a defendant has the right to question witnesses who may have information material to his or her defense. One witness, Ramzi Binalshibh, was charged with Moussaoui as a coconspirator in the September 11 hijackings, making access to him even more germane to Moussaoui's defense. Judge Brinkema, appointed by President Bill Clinton, had by this time agreed with Moussaoui that the statements of the three witnesses whom the government was holding in undisclosed locations could either bolster his defense or save him from the death penalty.

The government's refusal to make witnesses available was grounded in what it argued was the president's prerogative to protect national security in a time of war. Prosecutors argued that making the witnesses available would interfere with the government's interrogation of the witnesses for intelligence purposes. The defense attorneys wanted the case dismissed because, they argued, they needed the witnesses to exculpate Moussaoui, in whole or in part, of being complicit in September 11—the major thrust of the government's case against him. They argued, and Judge Brinkema agreed, that Moussaoui has a right under the Sixth Amendment to call witnesses in his defense.

In October 2003 Judge Brinkema shocked the prosecution and the defense. As sanction for the government's refusal to produce witnesses whom she felt might prove Moussaoui was not connected with September 11, she said the government could not mention September 11 in the case or try to tie Moussaoui to it. Since she had seen no evidence that he ever participated in any terrorist act or conspiracy to commit terrorism, she said that the government could not seek the death penalty. Stunned prosecutors appealed her ruling to the Fourth Circuit Court of Appeals, which heard argument in December 2003.[3]

At the oral argument, federal public defender Frank Dunham, lead defense attorney for Moussaoui, argued that not to enforce the law in the prosecution of Moussaoui because of the nature of the allegations against him said far more about our government than it did him, and that this would set a dangerous precedent for any defendant whom the administration thought undeserving of constitutional protections. The government argued, very simply, that the courts had no business telling the administration how to treat a defendant in a case connected with the war on terrorism. The judges seemed to suggest a middle ground—the witnesses would not be produced for the defense team, but the government would summarize what the witnesses knew. This would be unacceptable, Dunham said, for it plainly violates the Sixth Amendment right to cross-examine witnesses. Whatever the Fourth Circuit decides, still pending at the time this book went to press, the losing party will likely seek review in the U.S. Supreme Court. At any time, however, the government could remove Moussaoui from the jurisdiction of the federal courts by naming him an "enemy combatant." (See afterword for update.)

The twists and turns of the Moussaoui case illustrate a great irony. This prosecution would, according to U.S. attorney general John Ashcroft, demonstrate that alleged terrorists could get a fair trial in a U.S. court. Indeed, that is why the government chose to charge Moussaoui in Alexandria, rather than cage him in a military brig in Guantanamo Bay, Cuba, label him an enemy combatant, and forget about him or try him in secret before a military tribunal and then execute him. After all, the government later locked up Yaser Hamdi and Jose Padilla as enemy combatants, and they were American citizens. So why put Moussaoui, a French citizen, on trial in Alexandria? No one can say for sure, but a good guess is that Ashcroft had banked on getting a judge in the conservative Eastern District of Virginia to run the trial his way. Instead, Ashcroft and local prosecutors drew independent-minded Brinkema. She had served as a prosecutor in the district for years before she was a judge, but she had one guiding principle: she believed that the Constitution and Federal Rules of Criminal Procedure should apply to all criminal cases in her courtroom. She was not going to rewrite either document on an ad hoc basis just because those actions would have served Ashcroft's purposes.

The unraveling of the Moussaoui case is but one example of the unexpected setbacks the government suffered as it tried to lock up so-called terrorists. Though the appellate courts handed the government some stunning victories, sometimes the government's claims failed to pass the scrutiny of judges and juries, and the government had to settle for pleas to lesser offenses. Yet, to hear Ashcroft and Federal Bureau of Investigation (FBI) director Robert Mueller tell it, the government was winning its war in the courts hands down. (See afterword for further updates on this case.)

The Moussaoui case was not the first terrorist trial in Alexandria, Virginia, home of the "rocket docket" (a euphemism for the speed with which cases are tried or otherwise resolved). Nor would it be the last. Bracketing the Moussaoui case was the first trial of an American for alleged terrorism activities post–September 11, that of the so-called American "Taliban" John Walker Lindh, and a collection of cases against the "Alexandria Eleven," a supposed terrorist cell working in the backyard of the federal court. (See afterword for update.)

American Taliban: John Walker Lindh

Though he has never actually taken credit for it, Osama bin Laden is generally believed to be the mastermind behind the September 11 terrorist attacks. On that date, it is believed that he was in Afghanistan under the protection of the Taliban. The Taliban had gained control of the country from factional and regional warlords. President George W. Bush ordered the Taliban to turn over Bin Laden after September 11. When it did not, the United States began its war against the Taliban in October 2001. In January 2002 the United States formally declared that it had defeated the Taliban, even though it had not captured the Taliban's leader, Mullah Mohammed Omar, and American troops were still stationed in the country—and still are at the time this book went to press.

On February 5, 2002, Attorney General Ashcroft gave a press conference to announce an indictment by an Alexandria grand jury. This was a practice he would follow consistently with any terrorist-related indictment. With great bombast, he said that the ten-count indictment against the twenty-one-year-old John Walker Lindh charged him with "dedicating himself to killing Americans" and conspiring "to murder United States citizens." Ashcroft accused Lindh of "taking up arms" to hurt America and even accused him of complicity in September 11.[4] The pertinent facts, taken verbatim from the indictment, allege the following:

> After learning about the terrorist attacks against the United States on or about September 11, 2001, Lindh remained with his fighting group. Lindh did so despite having been told that Bin Laden had

ordered the attacks, that additional terrorist attacks were planned, and that additional al Qaeda personnel were being sent from the training camps to the front lines to protect Bin Laden and defend against an anticipated military response from the United States. From on or about October through early December 2001, Lindh remained with his fighting group after learning that United States military forces and United States nationals had become directly engaged in support of the Northern Alliance in its military conflict with Taliban and al Qaeda forces. On or about November 2001, Lindh's fighting group retreated from Takhar to the area of Kunduz, Afghanistan, and ultimately surrendered to Northern Alliance troops. On or about November 24, 2001, Lindh and other captured fighters were trucked to Mazar-e Sharif, in Afghanistan, and then to the nearby Qala-i Janghi (QIJ) prison compound. On or about November 25, 2001, Lindh was interviewed in the QIJ compound by two Americans, CIA employee Johnny Michael Spann and another United States Government employee, who were attempting to identify al Qaeda members among the prisoners. On or about November 25, 2001, Taliban detainees in the QIJ compound attacked Spann and the other employee, overpowered the guards, and armed themselves. Spann was shot and killed in the violent attack. After being wounded, Lindh retreated with other detainees to a basement area of the QIJ compound. The bloody uprising took several days to suppress. [5]

The indictment's allegations were dramatic, but as was typical of the government in post–September 11 cases, the charges were distortions of the truth. In reality, Lindh said he had gone to Afghanistan because, as a student of Islam he wanted to join the Taliban in fighting against the Northern Alliance. (The Taliban arose from an association of Afghan Muslim extremists who grew up mostly in Pakistani refugee camps, which they had fled to when Afghanistan was under Soviet occupation. With the help of Bin Laden and the government of Pakistan, they began to gain control

over most of Afghanistan beginning in 1994, after the loose association of warlords known as the Northern Alliance, which had
gained control of a large part of the country after the Soviets pulled
out in 1989, began to fall apart.) Lindh spent some time during the
summer of 2001 at an al Qaeda training camp (which was visited by
Bin Laden), but this was before the United States was involved in
Afghanistan and before September 11. He was captured in a training camp in November 2001, after the United States began the war
against Afghanistan. There was never any proof—and he and his
parents vehemently denied the allegations to the contrary—that he
wanted to kill Americans or that he was involved in the September
11 terrorist attacks.

Some argued that the government did not charge Lindh harshly
enough. Douglas Kmiec, former dean of Catholic University Law
School and legal counsel to presidents Ronald Reagan and George
H. W. Bush, criticized Ashcroft for not charging Lindh with the
crime of treason.[6] But treason was beyond the pale of even this
attorney general. Article III, Section 3 of the Constitution defines
treason as consisting "*only* in levying war against the United States,
or in adhering to their enemies, giving them aid and comfort."
Maybe the failure to charge Lindh with treason was a testimony to
the unusual nature of the crime with which Lindh was charged. He
was involved with the Taliban, but was he waging war against the
United States? There were doubts as to when Lindh knew that the
United States was at war with the Taliban. Further constitutional
constraints would have made a treason charge difficult. Article III,
Section 3 has an evidentiary requirement: "No person shall be convicted of treason unless on the testimony of two witnesses to the
same overt act, or on confession in open court." Lindh made con-
fessions, but not to treason. If Ashcroft thought of charging Lindh
with treason (and there is no evidence that he had done so), there
would have been the problem of calling credible witnesses to Lindh's
bearing arms against the United States. In the final analysis, not
charging Lindh or anyone else with treason can be attributed to the

strong and clear constitutional requirement for the charge, as well as the obviously weak connection between the war on terror and a traditional war fought with a foreign government—such as Germany in World War II.

The indictment against Lindh was carefully crafted to allow for multiple life sentences if he were convicted as charged. Later in the proceedings, the government toyed with the idea of charging Lindh with the killing of special forces agent Spann, since Spann was killed during a shoot-out at an Afghan prison where Lindh was temporarily held. There was no evidence that Lindh fired any shots, but the government could have tried to convict him on circumstantial evidence. The government raised the stakes by saying that they would seek the death penalty for Lindh if they charged him with Spann's murder. Spann's wife and parents lived in the northern Virginia area, and they joined the drumbeat to avenge their loved one's death with the execution of young Lindh. The government never did actually charge Lindh with the murder of Spann, though it did, until the very end, try to link him with Spann's death by innuendo and suggestion.

The pretrial proceedings in the Lindh case focused on several legal and factual issues. The most telling, however, had to do with whether or not Lindh's statements to FBI agents had been coerced or otherwise obtained in violation of his rights under *Miranda v. Arizona*. That case, father to the so-called Miranda rights, held that people held in custody by law enforcement personnel needed to be told prior to being interrogated that they have the right to be silent and to have an attorney present if they choose to speak.

Lindh was held offshore in a Navy vessel, often in a cargo container. Pictures of him bound and caged circulated throughout the press. Lindh's well-to-do parents, upon knowledge of their son's capture, retained the services of respected criminal defense attorney James Brosnahan. Lindh's parents and Brosnahan tried repeatedly to contact the FBI and instruct them not to question Lindh without the presence of his attorney. These communications were ignored, and Lindh's statements and his interview with a CNN reporter made up the heart of the government's case against him. Lindh had no access to his attorney until he was brought to the United States and incarcerated in Alexandria, Virginia, while awaiting trial.

Lindh was charged with conspiracy to murder U.S. citizens or U.S. nationals; two counts of conspiracy to provide material support and resources to designated foreign terrorist organizations; two counts of providing material support and resources to terrorist organizations; and one count of supplying services to the Taliban. Convictions could have led to multiple life sentences and six additional ten-year sentences plus thirty years. The government accepted Lindh's plea of providing services to the Taliban and possessing a weapon while doing so. But for that, Lindh also paid a high price—twenty years in prison. The stiffness of the sentence suggested the dilemma that terrorist defendants—and their attorneys—would face. Would they risk conviction, and even harder time, on more serious counts by going to trial?

As cases wound their way through the courts, this became a trend. The government failed, in many cases, to get any pleas to terrorist charges, but accepted pleas to lesser charges in exchange for prison terms that were harsh for the crimes pleaded to. Details that came to light after the Lindh plea agreement suggested that the actions of a young Justice Department attorney, Jesselyn Radack, led to the unraveling of the government's case against Lindh. For her part, Radack would become another victim in the war on terrorism as it was waged in the courts (see chapter 3).

Terrorist Cells

The U.S. government has disrupted terrorist cells in Buffalo, Seattle, Detroit, and North Carolina, and alleged terrorist cells in Portland and Tampa. In Buffalo, six U.S. citizens recently pleaded guilty

to providing material support to al Qaeda and admitted to training
in al Qaeda–run camps in Afghanistan. In Seattle, Ernest James
Ujaama pleaded guilty to providing material support to the Taliban. In Portland, seven individuals were charged with engaging in
a conspiracy to join al Qaeda and Taliban forces fighting against
the coalition in Afghanistan. Two individuals in Detroit were convicted of conspiring to support Islamic extremists plotting attacks
in the United States, Jordan, and Turkey. In North Carolina,
members of a cell who provided material support to Hizballah [sic]
were convicted, with the lead defendant sentenced to 155 years in
prison. In Tampa, Florida, eight individuals were indicted for their
alleged support of the Palestinian Islamic Jihad (PIJ). In Northern
Virginia, 11 men were indicted for conspiring to violate the Neutrality Act and firearm laws based on their participation in mili-
tary-style training in the United States and travel by several of the
defendants to Lashkar-e-Taiba (LET) camps in Pakistan in preparation for conducting violent jihad in Kashmir and elsewhere.

—From the WHITE HOUSE PROGRESS REPORT on the Global War
on Terrorism, September 2003 [7]

In a White House report issued on the second anniversary of
September 11, the Bush administration claimed victory over "terrorist cells" in Buffalo, Seattle, Detroit, and North Carolina. The
report claimed that of the 260 individuals charged with acts of terrorism, it had convicted or secured guilty pleas from over 140.
"Using authorities provided by the USA Patriot Act, the Department of Justice, working with other departments and agencies, has
conducted its largest investigation in history, thwarting potential
terrorist activity throughout the United States," the report stated.
This statement does not tell the true tale, however. In fact, the government successes consisted mostly of guilty pleas to lesser charges
than those alleged. A convenient catch-all charge was "providing

material support" to terrorist organizations. This could mean almost anything that the government wanted it to mean—from attending a mosque where men were called to jihad, to attending an al Qaeda training camp prior to September 11, to supporting Islamic charities. As we have seen, by the end of 2003, one federal court, the liberal Ninth Circuit Court of Appeals in California, had ruled that the material support statute was unconstitutionally vague, although the Bush administration is appealing the ruling.

At the time this book went to press, only one prosecution of an al Qaeda "cell," one in Detroit (see below), had gone to a jury. In that case, the government received a mixed verdict, and even that verdict has been cast into doubt by events revealed after the trial, which are discussed later in this chapter. The White House Report's reference to a North Carolina "cell" was somewhat misleading. It is true that in June 2002 a North Carolina federal court jury convicted two brothers of Lebanese descent of being part of a larger cigarette smuggling ring operating out of North Carolina, a source of inexpensive tobacco products. Chawki and Mohamad Hammoud were convicted of smuggling cigarettes from North Carolina to Michigan, selling them for a profit, and sending some of the money to Lebanon to support Hezbollah, an organization associated with numerous terrorist attacks in the Middle East. The investigation into cigarette smuggling had begun in 1996, but when it came to light that the money might be funneled to the Middle East, the men were charged with providing material support to an organization on the State Department's terrorist list. (See afterword for updates.)

THE LACKAWANNA SIX

In September 2002 six men, U.S. citizens of Yemeni descent, were arrested in Lackawanna, New York, and charged with "operating" an al Qaeda cell. Specifically, they were charged with providing material support to terrorists. It was alleged, and they later admitted, that they went to an al Qaeda training camp in Afghanistan in the spring of 2001, returning home in June. All men eventually pleaded guilty to the charge and received sentences of six and one-half to nine years. There was never any evidence that they took up arms against Americans or that they were planning any attacks on the United States. They had been receiving weapons training in Afghanistan in the spring of 2001, where they allegedly heard an anti-American speech by Bin Laden. The community was shocked, since the young men had grown up, were schooled, and worked in the community. Their supporters decried the prosecution, noting that they were responding to the call of jihad—not against the United States but in support of the Muslim cause against the Afghan warlords.

Investigative journalists from the *New York Times* and the PBS television series *Frontline* delved into the administration's allegations that the Lackawanna men were a terrorist cell and discovered that, as was the pattern in the Ashcroft Justice Department, the press releases and administration claims were horribly overblown.[8] The young men were hardworking men whose families were an integral part of the Yemeni American community. They had fallen under the spell, it seems, of a fundamentalist preacher, Kamal Derwish, at a Lackawanna mosque. For reasons not entirely clear, the government dropped its indictment against Derwish, and he was one of the victims in a car bombing in Yemen in 2002 that many believe to have been orchestrated by the Central Intelligence Agency (CIA). Though government officials have not confirmed that they arranged the attack, they admit that they will target terrorists through assassination attempts.

The federal prosecutor who headed up the investigation, Michael Battle, said that he did not consider the men terrorists, for he had no evidence of any plan or intent to do harm. Nor would he refer to them as a "cell," for he uncovered no concerted plot or conspiracy.[9] Prior to the USA Patriot Act, the FBI could not have detained the men because there was no probable cause to believe that they had committed a crime. But Ashcroft had called for the changes wrought by the Patriot Act precisely, in his view, for people like this. As Ashcroft had said repeatedly after September 11, the country cannot wait for terrorism "to happen;" we must prevent first and prosecute later.[10]

After September 11 the push was to find people responsible for the events of that day. The FBI in Buffalo was looking for Saudi Arabians who might have been involved in the September 11 attacks. But their attention turned to the Lackawanna men when a then-anonymous tipster alleged that they had attended an al Qaeda training camp. When first asked about this allegation, the men lied and said they went to Pakistan. When one of their group broke ranks and told the truth, the FBI arrested all the others. There was nothing but the tip in the anonymous letter to support the claim that the men had done anything except go to Afghanistan. By spring 2002 the case against the Lackawanna "cell" was progressing slowly. But then a man who had been captured fleeing Afghanistan and was imprisoned in Guantanamo Bay, Cuba, as an enemy combatant said that a terrorist cell was active in Buffalo. According to investigators on the case, this information seemed to confirm the anonymous tip sent to the FBI early in 2001. The FBI ramped up activities and ultimately assembled two hundred law enforcement agents from fifty agencies to descend on the Buffalo area and rout the sleeping cell.

Attorney General Ashcroft, FBI Director Mueller, and President George W. Bush were set on nailing the Lackawanna Six. Bush was briefed twice a day on the progress of the case. Were Americans plotting an attack? Was there enough evidence to charge them in criminal court? Heavy surveillance was undertaken of the seven men (which then included Derwish), pursuant to Foreign Intelligence Surveillance Act (FISA) warrants. E-mail intercepts from one of the men who was still abroad were interpreted in the most sinister fashion. He was writing about a wedding—and the FBI and CIA took that to mean a terrorist event. Actually, the man was getting married, and an FBI agent was sent to question him on the night before his wedding. Communications intercepted from this man, however, confirmed that the men had been in Afghanistan.

That the men had been in Afghanistan and lied about it was all that the government needed to issue indictments. By September 16, 2002, all of the men except Derwish had been charged with providing material support to terrorists. The Lackawanna case was hailed as victory in Bush's State of Union Address in January 2003. "We've broken al Qaeda cells in . . . Buffalo, New York," Bush said. "We have the terrorists on the run."[11] Mueller said the Lackawanna case was a significant win in the war on terror, largely due to the intelligence sharing between the CIA and FBI authorized by the Patriot Act.

Why did the men plead guilty to the charges, since they had done nothing wrong except lie about going to Afghanistan before the September 11 attacks? The prosecutors and the men's attorneys agree that the government's implied threat was that they would either be charged with "training with weapons" at a terrorist camp, for which they would receive thirty years, or, worse, be named by Bush as enemy combatants, carted off to a military prison, and never be heard from again.[12] Their attorneys were disappointed in their clients' decisions to plead, but they could not blame them for not taking a chance with their lives.

So, even though the Lackawanna Six were never tied to any terrorist acts or plans, to this day, Ashcroft, Bush, Mueller, and national security advisor Condoleezza Rice talk about shutting down the terrorist cell in Buffalo. And what the government did in the Lackawanna case became its modus operandi in virtually all terrorist trials: find people who appear to be suspicious; make them testify in front of a grand jury; try to find something they have done wrong; charge them with the maximum offense possible, making sure that one such charge is terrorist-related (for maximum fear value); convince the judge that the defendants are terrorists and thus have to remain in jail pending their trials (almost none of any defendants ever got out on bail, although there was never any evidence that any defendant was a danger to the community or a flight risk, the sole legal reasons for denying bail); and get one or two people to say something the government wants to hear, something to justify the prosecutions. Then, the prosecutors just had to wait for the men, sitting in jail in solitary confinement, to get scared and plead. That is precisely what happened in Buffalo. Ashcroft now had a winning strategy that would net huge political benefits.

According to *Washington Post* New York bureau chief Michael Powell, "The Lackawanna case illustrates how the post–September 11, 2001, legal landscape tilts heavily toward the prosecution. Future defendants in terror cases could face the same choice: plead guilty or face the possibility of indefinite imprisonment or even the death penalty. That troubles defense attorneys and some legal scholars, not least because prosecutors never offered evidence that the Lackawanna defendants intended to commit an act of terrorism."[13] There would seem to be little difference between the threat of indefinite imprisonment and physical coercion, but the law does not see it that way.

As tough as the prosecutors are, though, they don't call the shots. Ashcroft must be consulted in all trials of so-called terrorists, and no deals are made without his approval. It's tough justice— as tough as it gets—for Muslim men. Sentencing hearings of the men began on December 3, 2003, in federal court in Buffalo. The defendants generally received sentences of seven to ten years, based on their promise to fully cooperate with the government. Ironically, the day the first defendant was sentenced, the U.S. Court of Appeals for the Ninth Circuit ruled that the statute under which they were charged and pleaded was unconstitutional. (See chapter 5 for a discussion of this ruling.) Their cases were not affected by that court's ruling but could be if the U.S. Supreme Court eventually makes a similar determination.

Police presence and surveillance continue in Lackawanna. Citizens ask if there are any limits on who can be investigated. Indeed, Mohammed Albanna, a leader in the Yemeni community and an owner of a convenience store, has been charged with "illegally" transferring money to Yemen. The government suggests that he is laundering money for terrorists. He says he was sending money to his family and friends in his home country. Critics of the Lackawanna prosecutions suggest that if the government wanted to find out more about terrorist activity in this country, it could have used the men as intelligence tools rather than imprisoning them. Now, widespread distrust of the government has spread from Arab communities in Lackawanna to communities throughout the rest of the country. The government will find few willing to talk for fear of being prosecuted themselves.

THE DETROIT CELL

On June 3, 2003, a Detroit jury handed the government a mixed bag of verdicts: two acquittals and two convictions in charges brought against Arab men for providing material support for terrorists intent on attacking American and Middle Eastern targets. Specifically, the defendants were charged with looking for security gaps at Detroit International Airport, helping people make fake documents in order to gain entry into the United States, and recruiting members for a radical Islamist group with ties to al Qaeda. In this, the first al Qaeda–cell case that went to a jury, Moroccans Abdel-Ilah Elmardoudi and Karim Koubriti were found guilty of conspiracy to provide material support to terrorists and of conspiracy to engage in fraud and misuse of visas, permits, and other documents. Farouk Ali-Haimoud was acquitted of all charges, and Ahmed Hannan was acquitted of conspiracy to support terrorism but found guilty of conspiracy to engage in visa fraud, a lesser charge.

All four entered the country legally and at some point worked at the Detroit Metropolitan Airport. The case began with a raid on a

Detroit apartment just six days after the September 11 attacks. When federal agents searched the defendants' Detroit rowhouse, they seized a home video that the FBI said was of potential targets in Las Vegas, New York, and Disneyland. The FBI said sketches showed a U.S. military base in Turkey and a military hospital in Jordan. Agents found no weapons or explosives.[14] After the verdicts were handed down, the U.S. attorney's office in Detroit issued a press release typical in all of these cases, claiming full victory for the government.[15] But the case took a strange twist in December 2003. Prosecutors admitted that they had withheld information from defense attorneys that may have benefited the defendants. The defense attorneys asked U.S. District Court Judge Gerald Rosen to set aside the jury verdicts and grant their clients new trials. New prosecutors (the former prosecutors were removed from the case), however, say that the evidence, which centered on the credibility of one of the government's key witnesses, Youssef Hmimssa, would not have altered the verdict and a new trial is therefore not warranted.[16]

A prisoner sent a letter to prosecutors saying that Hmimssa bragged about lying to law enforcement in order to get a better deal in his own case. Hmimssa, a Moroccan national who was in the United States illegally, was convicted of three counts of fraud in a document and credit card scheme that netted more than $180,000 profit. He was incarcerated and awaiting sentence. Defense attorneys argued at the trial that Hmimssa testified falsely about the defendant's alleged scheme in order to get a lighter sentence. Prosecutors admitted that they had the letter in December 2001, but did not turn it over to defense attorneys. Failure to do so violates prosecutors' obligations to turn over to defense attorneys any information that is exculpatory in nature, meaning that it might undermine the prosecution's case and help the defendant. During the trial, Ashcroft violated Judge Rosen's gag order when he made public statements to bolster Hmimssa's credibility shortly before he testified in the trial. If Judge Rosen finds that the evidence should have been turned over, he could order a new trial, but he had not done so at the time this book went to press. At the hearing in which the defendants asked for a new trial, Judge Rosen expressed anger at the conduct of the prosecutors, who, it appears, willfully failed to turn over the evidence.[17] (See afterword for updates.)

THE SEATTLE CELL

The allegation that the government had broken up a terrorist cell in Seattle was likewise overblown. Several men who attended a Seattle mosque were charged with providing material support to terrorists. On April 14, 2003, the government extracted a plea from James Ujaama, an American convert to Islam. In exchange for his providing cooperation to federal authorities in an investigation of Abu Hamza al-Masri (a high-profile former imam at the allegedly radical Islamist Finsbury Park mosque in London), he will serve two years in prison.[18] Ujaama had faced the usual array of charges that the government brought in almost all such cases, the most serious of which was conspiring to kill Americans abroad and the least of which was providing material aid and support to a terrorist organization. Ujaama admitted to running Web sites for Abu Hamza and to being critical of U.S. foreign policy, and he pleaded guilty to one count of conspiring to provide cash, computers, and fighters to the Taliban. Several others charged in the so-called Seattle "cell" case had charges dropped in exchange for cooperating with the government. (See afterword for updates.)

THE PORTLAND SEVEN

The search for terrorist cells netted seven suspects in Portland, Oregon. Typically, all were charged with several offenses, the most serious being conspiring to kill Americans (which carries a life sentence) and to levy war against the United States. All of the defendants, including two brothers, Ahmed and Muhammad Bilal, eventually pleaded guilty to illegally possessing firearms—the government throws this charge into the indictments of almost anyone it thinks has a gun in his or her possession because it carries a mandatory ten-year prison term, even if the gun is legal in the state where the person is charged—and to "conspiring to help" al Qaeda and the Taliban during the war in Afghanistan. But what did the Bilal brothers actually do? Not much. They traveled to China with the other men charged, shortly after the September 11 terrorist attacks, and tried to gain entry to Afghanistan. They never made it to Afghanistan. Yet, in exchange for the government dropping the charge that could have sentenced them to life in prison, they admitted in their plea agreements that they "were prepared to take up arms and die as martyrs if necessary to defend the Taliban government in Afghanistan." As part of their deal with prosecutors, Ahmed Bilal agreed to a prison term of ten to fourteen years, while his younger brother agreed to eight to fourteen years.[19]

The case against the Bilal brothers and four other defendants was made possible partly due to the cooperation with the government of Intel software engineer Maher Hawash, a Palestinian-born naturalized American citizen. Hawash was seized from his home in the Portland, Oregon, area and held for months in an undisclosed location as a material witness. In exchange for his talking, the charge against him of conspiring to levy war against Americans was dismissed when he also pleaded guilty to conspiring to help al Qaeda and the Taliban. For planning to try to gain entry to Afghanistan, he is serving a seven-year prison term. Patrice Lamumba Ford and Jeffrey Battle also pleaded guilty and were each sentenced to eighteen years for conspiracy to levy war against the United States.[20] Battle's former wife, October Martinique Lewis, was convicted of wiring money to her husband and the other defendants.[21]

Hawash's case gained notoriety when he disappeared from his home and did not report to work for Intel. Friends and co-workers were shocked at the result. They could not imagine Hawash being involved in any terrorism. Nor was there any proof that he was a terrorist. Conspiracy charges are easy for the government to make—and that is why, if appropriate, most indictments contain a conspiracy count (e.g., conspiring to levy war against the United States) as well as charges of overt criminal acts (in this case, waging war against the United States with the Taliban). Any overt act to try to bring about an arguably unlawful action can be charged as a conspiracy. Still, the results for Hawash and his codefendants were draconian for people who never entered Afghanistan or took up arms against the United States. There would be other similar prosecutions with even fewer ties to terrorist acts. The members of the Alexandria Eleven would learn how little it took to be charged with crimes of terror. (See afterword for updates.)

THE ALEXANDRIA ELEVEN

In summer 2003 the federal courthouse in Alexandria, Virginia, saw another terrorism case. This one, also before Judge Brinkema, initially involved eleven men of Arab or Muslim descent. Some were American citizens. None of the men were initially charged with any terror-related crime. Instead, they were all charged with an arcane, rarely used law, the Neutrality Act, which forbids supporting any entity that is fighting a "friend" of the United States. The eleven men were charged with supporting Lashkar-e-Taiba, an organization placed on the State Department's list of terrorist organizations in December 2001. Lashkar opposes Indian control of the disputed Himalayan region of Kashmir, which has a mostly Muslim population. India and Pakistan had been warring over the region for years.

The government said that the prosecutions were part of the war on terrorism, claiming that Lashkar had connections to al Qaeda. Ashraf Nubani, a Virginia attorney representing one of the defendants, Randall Royer, said that taking the prosecutors' allegations to their logical conclusion would mean that "the whole Muslim world is involved with al Qaeda." [22] Nubani assailed the federal prosecutors for rounding up Arab men, "over" charging them, threatening them with even more serious charges, and then getting some to talk out of fear of merely having to defend against the charges.

Four of the Alexandria Eleven defendants allegedly told prosecutors that they were "preparing" to fight Muslim causes abroad in support of an organization labeled "terrorist" by the United States. They pleaded guilty to charges of "training" to take arms against an enemy of the United States, a violation of the Neutrality Act. Their "training" consisted of playing paintball, a wholly legal activity (and a popular activity for children and teens in the northern Virginia area). Two of the three sentenced at this time received prison terms of eleven and one-half years and four years. Judge Brinkema questioned the charges and the pleas, saying there was no proof that they ever intended to actually take up "arms" against anyone. Could they have been charged simply because they were Muslims? That is what Nubani thinks. Brinkema also expressed dismay that she had to sentence the men according to the mandatory federal sentencing laws, when their connection to terrorism was so weak. [23] (Unless there is evidence that a defendant is incompetent or cognitively impaired, a judge rarely looks behind the plea, other than to ascertain if it was voluntarily made. Voluntariness is strictly construed to mean that the defendant was not harmed or threatened with physical harm or made any overt promises in exchange for the plea. Unstated and implied threats do not render a plea involuntary.)

In January 2004 Royer, the resident of Falls Church, Virginia, who was charged as "ringleader" of the Alexandria Eleven, pleaded guilty to firearms charges, as did another defendant, Ibrahim Ahmed al-Hamdi. Al-Hamdi admitted that he was in a Lashkar camp in Pakistan in 2000 and learned how to use guns and grenades. Royer pleaded guilty to possessing a firearm in Virginia, which he said he used to prepare to fight at some future time. Virginia has liberal gun laws, and Royer's possession of a gun there was not a crime. But his admission that he possessed it in order to someday use it to fight with Lashkar qualified the possession as a crime. Royer is expected to receive twenty years in prison, al-Hamdi fifteen years. Royer will serve more time because he admitted that he recruited the others to support the Pakistani cause in Kashmir. In addition to the irony that Lashkar was not a banned organization at the time of their activities, in January 2004 India and Pakistan announced a cease-fire of hostilities relating to Kashmir and agreed to negotiate their dispute. (See afterword for updates.)

The Brooklyn Bridge Bomber

Iyman Faris, a thirty-four-year-old man of Pakistani descent who became an American citizen in 1999, pleaded guilty on May 1, 2003, to helping al Qaeda plan to bomb the Brooklyn Bridge. He later attempted to withdraw his plea, saying he was coerced into pleading guilty because the government threatened to declare him an enemy combatant and move him to Guantanamo Bay—unless he pleaded guilty to supporting al Qaeda and agreed to a twenty-year sentence. Judge Brinkema said she was satisfied that he was not coerced. This is not to say that he was guilty as charged, only that Judge Brinkema found his plea to be voluntarily made. In Faris's case, the judge reviewed all the evidence in secret, a growing practice in the federal courts. All the government has to do is allege national security interest for the courtroom doors to slam shut (see chapter 5). The public will never know what the evidence was against Faris, save what prosecutors chose to share. Faris said he had no connections with al Qaeda and that he initially cooperated with authorities so that he could get a "book deal." In the course of the year-long proceedings, he was off and on psychotropic medications and his mental health was called into question.[24]

The Terrorist Professor

In February 2003 the federal government handed down a fifty-count indictment against former University of South Florida computer science professor Sami Al-Arian. By the time his case goes to trial in 2005, he will have been under investigation for ten years and held without bond for more than two. Al-Arian, a forty-five-year-old father of five children, has lived in the United States for over twenty-five years. He made a name for himself as an outstanding computer engineering professor, eventually gaining tenure at the university. He was also a high-profile political figure in Florida, campaigning among Arab Americans for George W. Bush's presidential bid.

As with all the terrorist defendants, the charges against Al-Arian are impressive, to say the least. He, along with nine others, is being charged with heading the Palestinian Islamic Jihad in the United States and using a university think tank and Palestinian charity as fronts to raise money for terrorist attacks. Al-Arian has been shown to be planning nothing against or in the United States. His lawyer calls his indictment a "work of fiction." [25] Al-Arian says he is being targeted solely because he is an outspoken critic of the U.S. policies in support of Israel that are against the interests of Palestine and because he is influential in U.S. Arab communities. "I don't support suicide bombings," Al-Arian once said in a CNN interview. "I don't support the targeting of civilians of any nationality, background, or religion. I am deeply against it." [26]

The indictment alleges that Al-Arian wired tens of thousands of dollars to the Palestinian Islamic Jihad and to relatives of the group members jailed for their involvement in terror attacks in Israel and Gaza in the 1990s. Attorney General Ashcroft said, in a stock announcement he would use over and over about cases involving Islamic charities (discussed in chapter 4), "Those who finance terrorism are equal in guilt and equal in evil to those who direct and carry out terrorist attacks."[27] As in the case of the Lackawanna Six, the USA Patriot Act's provision that allows the FBI and the CIA to work hand in hand provided the ammunition for the indictment.

Amnesty International has denounced Al-Arian's solitary-confinement pretrial detention, in which he is shackled, chained, and exposed to bright lights day and night, as punitive and cruel. Phone contact is limited to one call to a family member for fifteen minutes a month. Attorney contact is restricted. Prison officials say he is being treated this way for his own protection. Al-Arian's trial is going to be a battleground for fights over the government's desire for secrecy and the defendant's constitutional right to a fair and open trial. Already, the trial judge, U.S. District Court Judge James Moody, has shown a leaning toward secrecy, ordering thousands of hours of surveillance tapes to be kept out of the hands of anyone except the government, the defendant, and the attorneys.[28] (See afterword for updates.)

Mohamed Atriss

Proving that state courts can violate constitutional rights as easily as federal courts, a state court judge in Patterson, New Jersey, locked up Mohamed Atriss for six months while he awaited charges of creating fake identity documents for alleged terrorists. For more than a year, Atriss did not know the evidence against him in order to be able to defend himself. The judge agreed with the prosecutors that the information should be kept secret to protect national security. When the transcripts of the secret hearings before Judge Marilyn Clark were unsealed, they were revealed to be replete with lies that purported to link Atriss with providing fake documents to two of the September 11 hijackers. The Passaic County Sheriff's Department said that they arrested Atriss on tips from the FBI. The

FBI, though, denied that they had authorized the raid of Atriss's home and office and his subsequent arrest. Prosecutors gave Judge Clark enough information to cause her to set Atriss's bond at $500,000, the amount that would be set for a first-degree murderer. Atriss appealed, and a state appellate judge found that there was not sufficient evidence of Atriss's being a national security threat to hold him on such high bond. Shortly thereafter, prosecutors folded and admitted that the only thing they had against Atriss was evidence that he sold some false documents to Hispanic immigrants.[29]

Atriss's case points out the horrible specter of American courts using secret evidence against American citizens, which it did in dozens of immigrant deportation cases and continues to do in pending terrorist trials. Secret evidence and secret trials are the most dangerous threats to our civil liberties. Secrecy is contrary to every basic tenet of the American criminal justice system—including due process, the right to a fair and public trial, and the right to face one's accusers (see chapter 5).

The Judiciary: Reluctant Arbiters in the War on Civil Liberties

The federal courts have many strengths, but the conduct of combat operations has been left to others. . . . The executive is best prepared to exercise the military judgment attending the capture of alleged combatants. The political branches are best positioned to comprehend this global war in its full context and it is the President who has been charged to use force against those "nations, organizations, or persons he determines" were responsible for the September 11 terrorist attacks. . . . The unconventional aspects of the present struggle do not make its stakes any less grave. Accordingly, any judicial inquiry into Hamdi's status as an alleged enemy

combatant in Afghanistan must reflect a recognition that government has no more profound responsibility than the protection of
Americans, both military and civilian, against additional unpro-
voked attack.

—*Hamdi v. Rumsfeld*, U.S. Fourth Circuit Court of Appeals, July
    12, 2002 [30]

The deference due to the Executive in its exercise of its war powers therefore only starts the inquiry; it does not end it. Where the
exercise of Commander-in-Chief powers, no matter how well
intentioned, is challenged on the ground that it collides with the
powers assigned by the Constitution to Congress, a fundamental
role exists for the courts.

—*Padilla v. Rumsfeld*, U.S. Second Circuit Court of Appeals,
    December 18, 2003 [31]

As the United States enters year four in the war on terror, the war
on civil liberties waged by the Bush administration enters year four
as well. To those who ask about the role of the courts in the war on
civil liberties, a good place to begin the explanation is with the
cases of Yaser Hamdi and Jose Padilla. For the petitions of these
two Americans reached two different federal circuits, both with
differing views of the role of the courts in the war on terror. The
court of appeals in the Hamdi case favors a judicial hands-off
approach to a president's wartime powers. The court of appeals in
the Padilla case believes that the president's powers do not exist in
a vacuum—they must comply with the law and the Constitution.

Hamdi and Padilla are both American citizens who have been
designated by President Bush as enemy combatants. The term
"unlawful combatant" is traditionally used to authorize the detention of hostile forces not wearing the uniform of a county, captured
on the battlefield and held in accordance with rules of war and

engagement. Typically, unlawful combatants would be tried by military tribunals, sent back to their countries, or executed, as was done in World War II in a case that came before the Supreme Court, *In re Quirin*. There, the Supreme Court reviewed the habeas petitions of German soldiers captured on United States soil during World War II. All of the petitioners had lived in the United States at some point in their lives and had been trained in the German army in the use of explosives. These soldiers, one of whom would later claim American citizenship, landed in the United States and shed their uniforms, intending to engage in acts of military sabotage. They were arrested in New York and Chicago, tried by a military commission as unlawful combatants, and sentenced to death. The Court denied the soldiers' petitions for habeas corpus, holding that the alleged American citizenship of one of the saboteurs was immaterial to its determination. But the *Quirin* case is not applicable to the current situation involving Hamdi and Padilla for several reasons. Among them is that the *Quirin* prisoners were German citizens who came to this country in order to sabotage the U.S. war efforts against their country, in a war with a known enemy. The prisoners were tried by a military tribunal. In contrast, Hamdi and Padilla have never even been charged with a crime.

YASER HAMDI

Yaser Hamdi is an American citizen who was captured in Afghanistan when the United States invaded that country after the September 11 terrorist attacks and it became the battleground for the war on terror. U.S. forces "captured" (this is the administration's term for it, though documents show that at least some of them surrendered to U.S. forces without a fight) almost 700 men and boys who were citizens of foreign countries (mainly Afghanistan and Pakistan, though a handful were from Great Britain, Australia, and other Arab countries) and shipped them to Guantanamo Bay, Cuba.

They were also named enemy combatants. Hamdi, however, was imprisoned at a navy brig in Norfolk, Virginia.

Enemy combatants were designated by the president, at the request of Secretary of Defense Donald Rumsfeld. Once the president designates prisoners as enemy combatants, they are in the formal custody of Rumsfeld, regardless of where they are imprisoned. They may or may not be tried, if they are ever charged. It's up to Rumsfeld and Bush to do as they please.

Hamdi was captured on a foreign battlefield —at least that is what the Pentagon says. Unlike the case of Padilla, in which the judge appointed attorneys, no judge appointed one for Hamdi. Why? Because, unlike Padilla, Hamdi was never actually in the jurisdiction of the court. Hamdi had been brought from Afghanistan, declared an "enemy combatant," and detained in a military prison.

With the support of Hamdi's family, Virginia Federal Public Defender Frank Dunham, who also represents Moussaoui, petitioned the court for access to Hamdi, who, being without funds for an attorney, would be entitled to the services of Dunham's office if he had been charged with a crime. Dunham challenged the status of Hamdi as an enemy combatant based on a two-page affidavit from Michael Mobbs, a Pentagon bureaucrat. The affidavit said that Hamdi was "affiliated" with a Taliban unit and received weapons training. It also says that he surrendered to Coalition forces—not that he was captured, as it commonly alleged in the press. The affidavit does not define what "affiliated" means, nor does it allege that Hamdi was fighting for the Taliban or that he was engaging in action against American forces.[32]

That challenge was heard by Robert Doumar, a judge of Middle Eastern descent. Doumar was incensed at the affidavit, which consisted of little more than conclusory statements. He was not willing to accept the affidavit of a Pentagon employee and without asking questions about how the employee reached these conclusions. Doumar wanted proof that Hamdi was actually seized in Afghanistan. How did Mobbs know that, he asked? And, if Hamdi was in Afghanistan, what did he actually have to do with the Taliban? "I'm challenging everything in the Mobbs declaration," warned Doumar. Where was the support for Mobbs's allegation that Hamdi was "affiliated with a Taliban unit"? And just what, Doumar begged, does it mean to be "affiliated" with the Taliban? Upon closer inspection, Doumar noted that the affidavit did not state that Hamdi was fighting with the Taliban, though that seemed to be what the government was suggesting in naming him an enemy "combatant." After all, what else does a combatant do but fight? The Mobbs document, Judge Doumar said bluntly, "makes no effort to explain what 'affiliated' means nor under what criteria this 'affiliation' justified Hamdi's classification as an enemy combatant. The declaration is silent as to what level of 'affiliation' is necessary to warrant enemy combatant status. . . . It does not say where or by whom he received weapons training or the nature and content thereof. Indeed, a close inspection of the declaration reveals that [it] never claims that Hamdi was fighting for the Taliban, nor that he was a member of the Taliban. Without access to the screening criteria actually used by the government in its classification decision, this Court is unable to determine whether the government has paid adequate consideration to due process rights to which Hamdi is entitled under his present detention." [33]

Shocked at the government's insistence that the Constitution did not apply to Hamdi and that the government could, in its own words, hold Hamdi incommunicado and without charge or trial "forever," Doumar ordered that Dunham have access to Hamdi in order to challenge the government's detention. The government, of course, promptly appealed and, in deference to the appellate court, Judge Doumar stayed his own ruling. When the Fourth Circuit handed down its opinion in the case of *Hamdi v. Rumsfeld*, it was clear that the court swallowed the government's argument

hook, line, and sinker. In an opinion that was more political argument than legal reasoning, the court gave the Bush administration
carte blanche to lock up American citizens indefinitely without
charging them with any crime and without access to an attorney,
based upon the conclusory statements of a government bureaucrat
who had no personal knowledge of the facts.[34]

To Doumar, that was an unthinkable assault on the heart of what
it meant to be an American—to have the protection of the Fourth,
Fifth, and Sixth Amendments. To the Fourth Circuit panel, it was
due deference to the executive branch of the government in a time
of war, even though this war may be a war without boundaries, and
without end.

In terms of the role of the courts in the war against civil liberties, the Fourth Circuit's decision that it would not interfere with
the president's prerogative on how to carry out a war states an
extreme position. Sitting in Richmond, Virginia, the most conservative federal appeals court in the United States simply took a
hands-off approach. It would not review any order of the president
naming an enemy combatant. It would not allow any enemy combatant to question the basis for his detention. It simply would not
interfere with the president's power to "conduct war." Citing the
great harm done to Americans on September 11, it resoundingly
gave the president full powers to conduct a war anywhere and under
whatever rules he wanted. To Hamdi's assertion that the fighting
in Afghanistan was over, the court said that the battlefield in the
war on terror could be anywhere in the world, anywhere the president said it would be. It would be, in effect, a moving battlefront.
That meant, by extension, that any American could be captured
anywhere, including on American soil, be named an "enemy combatant" if the president thought he or she were somehow engaged
in some manner of hostilities against the United States by word,
thought, or deed, and be imprisoned without access to any legal
remedy or judicial review.

Dunham has petitioned the Supreme Court to hear Hamdi's case. On December 2, 2003, in a move that seemed to be designed to better its position before the Supreme Court, the Pentagon announced that it would allow Hamdi to see Dunham. The change of heart was perhaps occasioned by criticism from former attorneys at the highest level of the Justice Department—Michael Chertoff, the chief terrorism prosecutor before he was appointed to be a judge on the Third Circuit Court of Appeals, and Viet Dinh, the major architect of the USA Patriot Act. They had begun to argue that the administration had gone too far in asserting that "detained" persons could be held by the government without counsel. The Pentagon said that it was making an exception by allowing this enemy combatant to have a lawyer and that its decision should not be construed as precedent for any other person so designated. Further, it said that it was only conceding that Dunham could see Hamdi, not that he could file a petition in a court and seek review of his enemy combatant status.[35]

On January 9, 2004, the Supreme Court announced that it would review Hamdi's case and take up the issue of whether an American citizen seized on a foreign battlefield and allegedly fighting against the United States could be designated as an enemy combatant and held without charge, trial, or attorney, merely on the president's order. The court heard arguments on April 28, 2004, and likely will render a verdict in June 2004. (See afterword for update.)

JOSE PADILLA: ANOTHER COURT SPEAKS

Jose Padilla is an American citizen who was captured in the United States—Chicago, to be exact. Originally, he was arrested and held as a material witness in a grand jury investigation based on his having been engaged in "loose talk" (in the words of prosecutors) about the possible detonation of a "dirty bomb," talk that prosecutors thought might be part of a conspiracy. He was not accused of engaging in any overt activity and, like Hamdi, has not been charged with a crime. The material witness statute is one that the government has used repeatedly since September 11 to hold "suspicious" persons for questioning. The use of the statute for this purpose has been widely criticized. Its original intent was to prevent a potential witness in a grand jury investigation or pending criminal case from fleeing the jurisdiction of the court and to keep a witness available for testimony. Some people have been held for as long as two years—and were still being held at the time this book went to press.

When Padilla was brought to New York, Judge Michael Mukasey appointed a New York City criminal defense attorney, Donna Newman, to represent him. Newman filed a petition challenging his being held in jail merely to testify before a grand jury. Judge Mukasey ruled that Padilla could be held as a material witness—a win for the government—but that he must be allowed access to his lawyer. Fearing that Newman would appeal Mukasey's ruling (which she did) while Mukasey put pressure on the government to allow Padilla to see Newman, federal prosecutors asked President Bush to name Padilla an enemy combatant and turn him over to Secretary of Defense Rumsfeld. The president did this, and so Padilla was moved from the jail in New York to a naval brig in Charleston, South Carolina, where he has been ever since, and held in solitary confinement. Before he was moved from New York, Newman had seen Padilla on several occasions.

Both Newman and the government appealed Judge Mukasey's ruling to the Second Circuit Court of Appeals: Newman challenged Padilla's enemy combatant status, and the government appealed the court's order that he have an attorney. The government claimed it had sufficient basis for Padilla's detention, a six-page statement by Pentagon official Mobbs, saying that Padilla had close associations with al Qaeda leaders as he traveled in Saudi Arabia, Afghanistan, and Pakistan over several years. Mobbs said that Padilla had trained in wiring explosives and that his plot to detonate a "dirty bomb" was in the early planning stages. In support of the designation, Bush said that Padilla was a continuing and grave danger to national security and that he had to be detained in order to prevent attacks against the United States. Several prestigious people and organizations, including former federal judges, filed friend of the court (amici) briefs in support of Padilla. They lambasted the authority the president claimed to detain Americans, which they contended were in violation of the most basic premises of American government—that citizens be afforded the protections of the rule of law and not be subject to the whim of an all-powerful executive branch.[36] The court found that President Bush had violated the 1971 Non-Detention Act, which forbids the government from detaining Americans without an act of Congress. The court rejected the government's contention that the Congressional authorization for a war on terrorism constituted an implicit override of the Non-Detention Act. Throughout history totalitarian regimes have attempted to justify their acts by designating individuals as "enemies of the state" who were unworthy of any legal rights or protections. These tactics are no less despicable, and perhaps even more so, when they occur in a country that purports to be governed by the rule of law.

On December 18, 2003, the Second Circuit Court of Appeals ruled that the naming of Padilla as an enemy combatant was unlawful. The court ordered the government to charge him with a crime, take him into custody as a material witness, or release him. The Bush administration, through Solicitor General Theodore Olson, said that it would not appeal the ruling to a full panel of the Second Circuit but would ask the U.S. Supreme Court to expedite its appeal in the case. Pending the administration's appeal to the Supreme Court, the court of appeals stayed its order that Padilla be charged with a crime or released. This means that Padilla will remain incarcerated, without access to counsel and incommunicado, until the Supreme Court acts. The Supreme Court heard the Padilla case on April 28, 2004. (See afterword for updates.)

RECONCILING THE HAMDI AND PADILLA CASES

In trying to reconcile these two cases, it is first important to recognize that they are different factually: Hamdi was captured on a foreign "battleground," Padilla on United States soil. Padilla was alleged to be associated with al Qaeda, and Hamdi with the Taliban. But beyond that, the cases differ vastly in the view that their respective courts took of their roles. The conservative Fourth Circuit took a fully deferential approach to the executive branch. It refused to act like a court. The Second Circuit, on the other hand, did just the opposite. Its opinion discussed in detail the concept of three coequal branches of government, each of which has a role to play in times of war and peace. It stated clearly that the president does not act in a vacuum—he acts according to law. It found no legal basis for the president's naming of Padilla as an enemy combatant.

The larger question, which the appellate court decision addressed and which may ultimately be answered by the U.S. Supreme Court, is whether or not an American citizen, arrested on United States soil, can be held incommunicado in a military prison indefinitely, without being charged with a crime and without access to a lawyer. "The [president's] constitutional argument [in the case of Jose Padilla] would give every President the unchecked power to detain, without charge and forever, all citizens it chooses to label as 'enemy combatants,'" says the Cato Institute, in a friend-of-the-court brief filed in the Supreme Court case of *Rumsfeld v. Padilla*.[37] The Center for National Security Studies, the Constitution Project, the Lawyers Committee for Human Rights, People for the American Way, and the Rutherford Institute joined the brief.

The Supreme Court

On April 20, 2004, the U.S. Supreme Court heard oral arguments in the cases of some of the enemy combatants held at Guantanamo Bay, Cuba (see chapter 5). Either the government or the aggrieved party in almost every case we discuss in this book may make its way to the Supreme Court for final determination. That does not mean that the Supreme Court will take the cases, however. In most cases, the Supreme Court's review is discretionary. It takes the cases it wants to take by granting what is called *certiorari*. Whether the Court will act independent of the Bush administration will, as usual, depend on the votes of two of the "swing" members, Justice Sandra Day O'Connor and Justice Anthony Kennedy, both conservatives with an independent streak. Chief Justice William Rehnquist's view is already clear. His 1998 book *All the Laws but One: Civil Liberties in Wartime* is a resounding tribute to the power of the executive during wartime, with particular emphasis on President Abraham Lincoln's suspension of the writ of habeas corpus during the Civil War. Though the Supreme Court held such an action unlawful because it required, in its opinion, an act of Congress, Lincoln ignored the Supreme Court. There was nothing (nor is there anything today) the Supreme Court could do to a president who ignores its orders. Rehnquist defends Lincoln's actions as being required to save the Union.[38]

Do We Have an Independent Judiciary?

We cannot be too optimistic about judges, since Congress has appointed almost all of President Bush's judicial nominees to trial and appellate courts. Those the Senate Judiciary Committee have rejected represent only the most extreme appointees, and they are only a handful. One hundred seventy-one Bush judges have been appointed (not counting the 2004 recess appointments of Charles Pickering and William Pryor, who had not been confirmed by the Senate at the time this book went to press), bringing Republican appointees (under President George H. W. Bush, Ronald Reagan, and George W. Bush) to 50 percent of the federal bench. If Bush is elected for a second term, the number of conservative judges will continue to grow, along with the possibility that several Supreme Court seats will become vacant. Whether the war on civil liberties will become a part of the larger war on crime, in which draconian sentences are meted out for minor offenses and we continue to build more prisons than schools, remains to be seen. In the war on crime, legislation and executive meddling have taken away much of the power of federal judges. For instance, long mandatory minimum sentences as mandated by Congress have tied judges' hands when it comes to trying to fashion the punishments that fit the crime and the person. Ashcroft's meddling in decisions about which courts try terrorist cases and what charges must be brought have further injected the executive branch of government into the judiciary. Thus, the judicial branch, in addition to what it may be giving up freely, is being further weakened by unwanted intrusions from the legislative and executive branches.

Then, too, there is the inescapable fact that for the past twenty years, courts have been complicit in eroding civil liberties in the context of criminal prosecutions. The constitutional guarantees against the right not to incriminate one's self and not to be subject to unreasonable searches and seizures are but a shadow of what they were in the 1960s, at the end of the most civil libertarian era the Supreme Court has ever seen, presided over by Justice Earl Warren. When lower courts have limited civil liberties, the Supreme Court has generally accepted these rulings. The only area that seems to have escaped intrusions from judicial constraint is pornography—the Supreme Court still upholds the rights of adults to consume pornography, while other speech rights have been limited.

There have been a handful of unusually independent judges—notably judges Brinkema and Doumar in the Eastern District of Virginia and Judge Mukasey in New York, neither of whom are soft on terrorism—who defer to the president because of the uniqueness of the war on terror and the horror of September 11. It seems clear that judges, like politicians and citizens, are letting the memory of that day cloud their dedication to protecting the Constitution and the rule of law. Yet without faithful adherence to the doctrine of the separation of powers, without legislators legislating with calm and deliberation (as was not seen in the passage of both the Patriot and Homeland Security acts) and judges judging with care and reason, President Bush has filled (and will fill) the power vacuum.

Judges cannot decide cases without lawyers. Defense attorneys such as Newman and Dunham battle federal prosecutors in the front lines of the war against civil liberties. As we will see in the next chapter, two attorneys—one a defense attorney and one a Department of Justice lawyer—became defendants in the war on terror. Both claimed that they were fighting to preserve the rule of law and the Constitution.

3

THE WAR AGAINST LAWYERS

Shortly after terrorists attacked the United States on September 11, 2001, the Department of Justice promulgated a rule creating the authority to monitor the attorney-client communications of federal inmates whom we suspected of facilitating acts of terrorism. . . . This afternoon, I am announcing the indictment of four associates of Sheikh Abdel Rahman . . . including Rahman's lawyer, a United States citizen—with aiding Sheikh Abdel Rahman in continuing to direct the terrorist activities of the Islamic Group from his prison cell in the United States.

—ATTORNEY GENERAL JOHN ASHCROFT, *October 9, 2002,*
announcing the indictment of New York criminal defense lawyer
Lynne Stewart. [1]

Taking on controversial clients charged with heinous crimes is always a risk for defense attorneys. In the immediate aftermath of September 11, lawyers who did this work were often looked upon as traitors. Now, taking "terrorist" cases is seen more along the lines of attorneys defending criminals whose crimes society finds abhorrent—that is what attorneys do. Nonetheless, the courageous lawyers who continue to take on these cases put their reputations on the line as they agree, most for court-appointed fees, some as public defenders, to represent defendants charged with having committed crimes of "terror" and immigrants detained and prosecuted in deportation proceedings—persons vilified by prosecutors and the press. But until the indictment of Lynne Stewart in April 2002, few would have realized that they themselves could be arrested simply for doing their jobs.

Lynne Stewart

On October 9, 2002, Attorney General John Ashcroft held a public news conference in the shadow of the ruins of the World Trade Center to announce the unprecedented indictment of a lawyer he described as a "terrorist." Sixty-four-year-old New York City criminal defense attorney Lynne Stewart was charged with four counts of aiding and abetting a terrorist organization. The indictment accused her and codefendants Ahmed Abdel Sattar (Stewart's translator, since she speaks no Arabic), Yassir al-Sirri, and Mohammed Yousry with staffing a "communications pipeline" between her client Sheik Abdel Rahman, the blind cleric convicted in 1995 of plotting to blow up New York landmarks such as the George Washington Bridge, and the Islamic Group, an organization that had claimed credit for the massacre of sixty-two people at an archeological site in Luxor, Egypt, in 1997. She was also charged with interfering with the prison's taping of her meetings with her client because she talked to herself or others in the meeting room so that the tape would not be clearly transcribable. Stewart took these actions, alleged the indictment, in order to help maintain Rahman's influence over the terrorist activities of the Islamic Group, an organization that had long been on the Treasury Department's list of terrorist organizations.

How was it that the government was able to record conversations between an attorney and her client? After all, attorney-client communications have, until the reign of Ashcroft, been subject to an ancient and sacrosanct rule of confidential privilege. This privilege used to mean that neither the government nor anyone else could make a lawyer or client disclose the content of their communications. On October 31, 2001, Ashcroft changed all that when, in the name of fighting the war on terror, he ordered the Bureau of Prisons (BOP) to begin audio recording of meetings between certain federal inmates and their attorneys. He had a short list at the time (only sixteen names). His order would be carried out "to the extent determined to be reasonably necessary for the purpose of deterring future acts of violence or terrorism." [2] According to its terms, prisoners and their attorneys would be told that their communications "might be" taped, but would never know whether or not they were actually recorded.

The October 2001 order was not Ashcroft's first attack on federal detainees' relationships with their attorneys. Before the eavesdropping regulation, Ashcroft and government prosecutors had begun to impose Special Administrative Measures (SAMs) on detainees, defendants, and convicts (whether pending their trials, during their trials, or when serving prison time after conviction).[3] These measures placed certain restrictions on the type and nature of conduct between those in custody and the outside world. For instance, some detainees would be denied visits from particular persons or denied mail or magazines from a particular source. This is not a particularly new concept, for prison officials have always had a lot of leeway in how they manage their prison populations. But what was unusual was two things: (1) the people on whom these measures were placed were chosen by Ashcroft and prosecutors, not prison officials within the BOP, and (2) more important, restrictions would be placed on attorneys, who would have to abide by them if they wanted access to their clients.

Traditionally, attorneys have had virtually unfettered access to their incarcerated clients. Very few limits are placed on the time and length of visits, and the visits are supposed to be protected from surveillance by prison officials. The SAMs allowed Ashcroft to define the parameters of the attorney-client contact—for instance, attorneys could not talk about anything except what fit within the scope of their representation. According to attorney ethical codes, a lawyer's duty to his or her client is very broad, from being a legal advocate in court to being a counselor and adviser. When Ashcroft took it upon himself to allow taping of attorney-client conferences taking place in the prisons, he became the arbiter of when an attorney had stepped beyond the line of proper content of attorney-client communications that he, Ashcroft, had drawn. When it came to attorney Stewart, Ashcroft determined from surveillance tapes and other circumstances that, in his view, Stewart had crossed this line.

As it turned out, the Justice Department had been monitoring communications between Stewart and her client, Rahman, for four years. It had access to Stewart because it was conducting surveillance on Rahman pursuant to a Foreign Intelligence Surveillance Act (FISA) warrant. Prior to the USA Patriot Act, an American citizen (such as Stewart) could not be the subject of a FISA warrant, but she was "collateral" damage. Stewart had been caught in the FISA trap. But it wasn't until April of 2002 that she knew this.

The arrest and indictment of Stewart sent chills down the spines of criminal defense attorneys. And the image of U.S. marshals raiding her offices and taking with them every file, computer, phone, and book therein had lawyers envisioning ruined practices and lost credentials. When the federal government raids an attorney's office, the state licensing authority takes notice. Beyond the issue of the security of client files, a client's ability to speak freely to his or her lawyer (and the attorney's ability to talk to his or her client) is an essential right. Having a client who is candid with his or her lawyer is a necessary corollary of the Sixth Amendment right to counsel. If the government can know what a client tells his or her lawyer, and what the lawyer advises, a defendant is conceivably at greater risk than if he or she went up against the government unrepresented. Some would argue that there can't even be an attorney-client relationship if the government is listening to everything said.

Ashcroft's attorney-client surveillance rule, like so many laws enacted in the name of fighting terror, was not a necessary step in thwarting criminal conduct between nefarious attorneys and their criminal clients. U.S. law has long recognized that attorney-client privilege of confidentiality does not protect communications that enable future illegal conduct. If prosecutors have reason to think that the attorney and client are engaging in criminal activity, they can obtain wiretap and search warrants from a federal judge. Of course, this old-fashioned and constitutionally sanctioned way of getting evidence means that the government has to have some showing that wrongdoing is afoot and must eventually disclose to the parties searched and taped the evidence garnered against them. Ashcroft devised a scheme that would circumvent all those constitutional details for clients in prison.

But the indictment of Stewart signaled that Ashcroft had plans to change the attorney-client landscape outside prison walls as well. Upon announcing the indictment, Ashcroft said:

> Since our country was attacked over six months ago, I have sought to reassure the American people that the actions of the Department of Justice are carefully designed to target terrorists and to protect American rights and freedoms. Today's actions pursue the same objectives with the same protections in mind. We will not look the other way when our institutions of justice are subverted. We will not ignore those who claim rights for themselves while they seek destruction for others. We will, in the President's words, defend freedom—and justice—no matter what the cost. [4]

Are the Sixth Amendment right to counsel and a lawyer's own First Amendment rights too high a cost? The issue would come before U.S. District Court Judge John Koeltl of the Southern District of New York. At Stewart's side would be famed litigator and preeminent civil liberties attorney Michael Tigar, himself no stranger to unpopular causes—and clients.

Stewart had a lifelong history of representing unpopular clients (most of them as court-appointed counsel), including those who belonged to such groups as the Black Liberation Army and the Weather Underground. But her most notorious client to date—and the reason she herself is facing the possibility of imprisonment—is Rahman. Stewart, convinced of Rahman's innocence, wept in court when the guilty verdict was handed down. Harsh restrictions limiting his ability to communicate with the outside world were imposed upon him. Stewart continued to meet with her client at the federal penitentiary in Minnesota. She was one of the few contacts he had with the outside world. A SAM limited his family visits to those of close relatives only, all of whom lived in Egypt and could not get visas to enter the United States.

After a prison visit to the sheik in 2000, Stewart answered a reporter's question about whether or not the sheik would support a cease-fire of belligerent activity against Americans abroad. (His organization was implicated in the 1998 bombings of U.S. embassies in Nairobi, Kenya, and Dar es Salaam, Tanzania, and was said to support continued attacks against the United States.) Stewart said that it appeared that he would not, given her communication with him. This event apparently made the government focus more closely on Stewart's communications with the sheik. For a period of time after this comment, Stewart was denied access to her client; visits resumed when she renegotiated a SAM with the BOP. Stewart would not have been allowed to see her client had she not agreed to abide by the SAM measures.

The first indictment's terrorism charges were dismissed by Judge Koeltl in July 2003. He ruled that the charges against her, if allowed to go forward, could punish any attorney for doing what he or she is bound to do—communicate with and about their clients. (She still faced charges that she violated the SAMs and lied to the government about her intention of abiding by them in the first place; the trial, originally set to begin in January 2004, was, at the time this book went to press, scheduled for May 2004.) New York lawyer Sam A. Schmidt, who defended Wadih el Hage, one of four men convicted in the 1998 bombings of the U.S. embassies in Kenya and Tanzania, echoed Judge Koeltl's concerns. He also had to sign a SAM and says he was troubled by it. Moreover, he says such agreements give lawyers little guidance on how their communications with clients cross the line and become crimes. "I try to follow the law, and I think I am following the law," Schmidt said. "But these things are so broad and vague that if the government wants to go against me, it can. It's frightening what they can do." [5]

The government was not to be deterred from prosecuting Stewart for terrorism. With the trial date only six weeks away, on November 19, 2003, the government handed down what is known as a "superseding" indictment against Stewart. It charged her with two new counts of aiding and abetting terrorism, using a different section of the Patriot Act. The new charges did not seem any better from a constitutional standpoint than the ones the judge dismissed. Whereas the first indictment focused on Stewart as a "personnel" of a terrorist organization (the organization her client was associated with), the new indictment charged her with using her statements and access to her client as a means of providing him as "personnel" to a terrorist organization. Laying aside legal semantics, those who had been keeping an eye on the tactics of Ashcroft's Justice Department recognized vengeance when they saw it. The government would stop at nothing to try to ensure that

Stewart would go to prison and, worse from her perspective, lose her law license. Time and again, the government's loss in a case has led it to strike at the defendant with new threats and new charges.

At the same time that Stewart was facing a superseding terrorism indictment, a young attorney was fighting her own battle against Ashcroft's vengeance.

Jesselyn Radack

In chapter 2, we discussed the case of "American Taliban" John Walker Lindh. The government had shown no signs of dropping its demand for multiple life terms for the young man Ashcroft claimed was conspiring to wage war against the United States and murder its citizens. But suddenly, on July 15, 2002, a plea agreement was announced. Lindh pleaded guilty to aiding the Taliban with the use of a weapon. The weightier terrorism charges of conspiring to kill Americans and to wage war against the United States were dropped—but Lindh would not get off easy. He agreed to serve twenty years in prison, to forgo any profits to media stories about his past, to abide by restrictions on his contact with his attorneys while incarcerated (the notorious SAMs), and to accept that if he is charged with any future crimes related to aiding an enemy of the United States he may be declared an "enemy combatant" (subjecting him to possible life imprisonment without charge or trial, and with no access to an attorney—ever).[6] Sometime after the plea, a story came to light that suggested that a young, idealistic Justice Department attorney, now a target of Ashcroft's wrath herself, may have had something to do with the unraveling of the government's case.

Jesselyn Radack is the thirty-two-year-old mother of three young children. A graduate of Yale University Law School, she was chosen for the prestigious Department of Justice Honors Program, which seeks to put promising attorneys on the fast track to the front lines of government law. At the time of Lindh's capture in December 2001, she was working in the Justice Department's Professional Responsibility Advisory Office, a special branch created by the department in 1999 to advise on potential ethics conflicts. The government in Afghanistan had just captured Lindh. In a series of e-mails, Radack advised John De Pue, a counterterrorism prosecutor, that since Lindh's father had hired attorney James Brosnahan, she didn't think the FBI could question Lindh outside the presence of his lawyer. The Department of Justice Terrorism and Violent Crimes Section was not convinced that the normal rules of interrogation applied to the Lindh situation. Radack's opinion was ruled out based on the rationale that the interrogation was taking place not in the United States but in Afghanistan. Lindh had been found fighting with the Taliban. And the context was war, not the typical criminal investigation.

As Lindh's case made its way to federal court in Alexandria, his legal team, led by Brosnahan, sought to suppress Lindh's statements to interrogators based on violations of Lindh's Miranda rights. Though Lindh did not know that he had an attorney to contact, it was clear that his parents and then his attorney tried to assert his Miranda rights in his stead. Brosnahan sought to discover what the FBI and Department of Justice knew about his efforts to contact them with requests to be present when Lindh was being interrogated. Judge T. S. Ellis III ordered that all Department of Justice correspondence about the Lindh interrogation be turned over to him.

In the course of preparing to comply with Judge Ellis's order, Assistant U.S. Attorney Randy Bellows contacted Radack by e-mail. Bellows said he wanted to be sure that he had all of Radack's e-mails to and from the counterterrorism prosecution unit. This request was the first time Radack had heard about the court order or that Bellows had any of her e-mails. But when she found out that he had only two e-mails between her and De Pue, she felt that something was "terribly wrong" because they had exchanged more than two e-mails about the case. She notified her supervisor, Claudia Flynn, who assured her that she sent Bellows everything that was "in the file." Radack, in a move she now admits was naive, said that she was sure there were more than two and that she would check into it. For she had meticulously saved all communications with Justice Department attorneys; after all, the advice from her office was, as she termed it, the attorneys' "get out of jail free card." In other words, Justice Department attorneys could rely on the counsel of her office, and her office would take the hit if FBI or Department of Justice employees made a legal error.

When Radack attempted to retrieve the e-mails from her computer, she found that they had been "purged." Some may have disappeared under standard procedures of being deleted after the passage of time, but others she felt had been deliberately removed. She wanted to make sure that all her communications reached the judge, so the confirmation that there were files missing led her to contact Donald McKay, a former U.S. attorney who was a personal friend. His advice to her was to call the computer help line and get them to help retrieve the e-mails, write a memo to Flynn, and attach the e-mails. Radack did just that and put the memo, with printed copies of the e-mails, on Flynn's desk chair.

Flynn's reaction surprised Radack. "Why weren't these in the original file sent to Bellows? Now I have to explain why everything did not get turned over." Radack reminded Flynn that she had nothing to do with searching for or turning over any e-mails to Bellows. But more was going on than missing e-mails. The week before this exchange, Flynn had given Radack a bad performance evaluation and suggested she start looking for another job outside the department. All prior evaluations had been excellent; she had even received special commendation from FBI director Robert Mueller. Radack never knew if or when Bellows received the missing e-mails.

Flynn told Radack not to contact Bellows, for reasons that Radack did not understand. But she naively thought that she ought to give the prosecutor what the judge had ordered be produced, and she feared that was not being done. So she contacted Bellows. In June 2002 Radack provided some of the e-mails to journalist Michael Isakoff, and he published them in a *Newsweek* article. A couple of weeks later, Lindh pleaded guilty.[7]

If that were the end of the story, Radack's tale would be that of just another idealistic and naive attorney who was disillusioned by the workings of the "real" world. But the Department of Justice opened a criminal investigation into Radack. Accused of violating department regulations about confidentiality and interfering with an investigation, she found herself fired from her subsequent job at a Washington, D.C., law firm. In September 2003 Radack was informed that the Department of Justice had "closed its file" on her.

The Department of Justice's treatment of Radack got the attention of Senator Edward Kennedy (D-MA). In the confirmation hearings of Michael Chertoff to sit on the Third Circuit Court of Appeals, Kennedy questioned Chertoff, then head of Department of Justice's criminal branch and De Pue's boss, about the controversy surrounding the Lindh interrogations and the treatment of Radack. Kennedy voted for Chertoff's confirmation, but not without making a public statement. Kennedy was concerned about "inconsistencies" in the responses Mr. Chertoff provided with respect to the debate over the legality of the interrogation of John Walker Lindh." Specifically, Chertoff did not tell the truth when he said that Radack's Professional Responsibility Advisory Office was not contacted about the propriety of questioning Lindh. When confronted with the e-mails that were published by *Newsweek*, Chertoff conceded that De Pue was involved, but that he was not a major player. Kennedy chided him for his lack of "candor." As for the treatment of Radack after the disclosure of her office's involvement in the Lindh matter, Kennedy expressed his displeasure that

Radack "was in effect fired for providing legal advice on a matter involving ethical duties and civil liberties that higher-level officials at the Department disagreed with. Furthermore, after Ms. Radack notified Justice Department officials that they had failed to turn over several e-mails requested by the federal court, Department officials notified the managing partners at Ms. Radack's new law firm that she was the target of a criminal investigation." [8]

The Department of Justice may have closed its criminal file on Radack, but, as with Stewart, Radack would learn in November 2003 that the government would not leave her alone. Having found no basis for a criminal charge, the Justice Department reported her to the states where she is licensed to practice law and requested that they conduct their own ethics investigations into her conduct. They say that she broke ethical rules by talking about the missing e-mails and the government's investigation of her.

It is unlikely that the state bar organizations will stand up to Ashcroft, who is breathing down their necks and looking to them for surrogate vengeance. After all, what might he do to them if they don't give him what he wants? But even if they do stand up to him, the fact that she was reported and an investigation was undertaken is one that will be on her record for years, and one she has to report to malpractice insurance carriers. At the time this book went to press, the disciplinary cases against her were pending and she was unemployed and unemployable.

Enemy Combatants and Their Lawyers

Thus far, in spite of erosions of some of the basic principles of practicing law in the United States, defense attorneys are standing firm in their fight to protect the freedoms guaranteed by the Constitution. In many cases, they do so handicapped by rules governing terrorist trials. Most must have security clearances to see evidence against their clients; some have no access to certain evidence because judges deem it to be against the interest of national security. They defend their clients the best they can.

As discussed in chapter 2, Federal Defender Frank Dunham persists in representing a client he has never seen, Yaser Hamdi. He is asking the U.S. Supreme Court to review the designation of Hamdi as an enemy combatant and to be allowed to represent him. In December 2003 the Pentagon relented and said that Dunham could visit Hamdi, but it did not concede that Hamdi could petition the court to challenge his enemy combatant status. Donna Newman and Andrew Patel persisted in representing their client, Jose Padilla, over an almost two-year period, until a federal appellate court ordered him released or charged as a criminal. Once Padilla was removed from a New York jail (where he was being held as a material witness; see chapter 2), his lawyers were denied access to him.

There were 675 (more or less, as the government gives scant and sporadic reports) men and boys initially imprisoned in Guantanamo Bay, Cuba, none of whom have seen a lawyer in the almost two years they have been there. As enemy combatants, the Pentagon says they don't get to see a lawyer unless and until the Pentagon tries them in military tribunals, the rules for which are constantly changing as the administration takes heat from civil libertarians and even some military lawyers and judges. Then, they will get a military lawyer unless they can afford a civilian lawyer. Even then, that lawyer must be approved by the Pentagon and must abide by strict rules of conduct that most attorneys believe violate attorney ethical codes, even the law protecting attorney-client confidentiality. The rules facing Guantanamo attorneys include: (1) they must obtain and pay for their own security clearances, and they cannot represent anyone without having clearance; (2) they must agree to never talk about anything they see, hear, or do while at the base unless it is pre-cleared by the Pentagon; (3) all of their contacts with their clients will be monitored and audio- and videotaped; (4) they will only be

allowed to see the evidence the Pentagon allows them to see; and
(5) some of their proceedings against their clients may take place
out of their presence, if the Pentagon deems it to be in the best
interest of national security. The value of having outside counsel
was demonstrated in the spring of 2004. Pro bono attorneys and
public interest legal organizations filed lawsuits against President
Bush and Secretary of Defense Rumsfeld challenging the detention
of several of the prisoners. The U.S. District Court for the District
of Columbia and the D.C. Court of Appeals rejected their petitions,
but the Supreme Court agreed to hear the case. The Court heard
oral arguments on April 20, 2004, and a decision is expected by the
end of the court's term in June 2004. Prior to the Supreme Court
hearing, five British detainees were released from Guantanamo and
returned to England. British authorities held them for a day and
released them, finding that they had committed no crime under
British law (whose antiterrorism statutes are even stronger than our
own). The men likely would not have been released, and their petitions certainly would never have been filed in federal court, had they
not had lawyers on the outside (most of whom had never even met
their clients) who pursued justice for them. One of the British prisoner's lawyers, Stephen Kenny, warned, as have civil libertarians in
this country, that the erosion of civil liberties in Guantanamo Bay,
particularly in regards to constitutional safeguards for criminal trials guaranteed by the Fourth, Fifth, Sixth, and Eighth Amendments, are but a harbinger of widespread changes in the legal system
for all Americans.[9] Certainly, those changes have come to those
people, mostly Muslims and Arabs, charged with crimes related,
however remotely, to "terror." (For more on Guantanamo Bay, see
chapter 5 and the afterword.)

For all the criticism leveled at attorneys in the United States, for all
the vilification dished out by the Bush administration and Ashcroft,

dedicated attorneys are all defendants have going for them when the government wants to try them with secret evidence or lock them up indefinitely without trials. These attorneys try to do their jobs and uphold the guarantees of the Constitution in spite of huge government restraints. Anthony Romero, executive director of the American Civil Liberties Union, said, "The Justice Department has had a very conscious policy since 9/11 of denying access to lawyers and, when they allow access, undercutting the detainees' right to counsel. It has been a clear and distinct policy of trying to limit attorneys at every turn." [10]

In spite of all the roadblocks put in the path of diligent attorneys, most have done a masterful job of defending so-called terrorists, only a few of whom have been convicted of overt acts of terrorism. This is both a testimony to the weakness of the government's cases and the tenacity of American lawyers. It is the lawyers who must try to ensure that the foundation of our laws—the Constitution—does not crumble, that the protections of the Bill of Rights will prevail in the face of fear, and that justice will triumph over tyranny.

In chapter 4 we examine the nigh impossible task of defending Muslim charities that the government alleged were aiding and abetting terrorism.

4

GUILT by ASSOCIATION

The Islamic Charities

Today we are blocking the assets of two organizations and two individuals who have been stealing from widows and orphans to fund al Qaeda terrorism. These bad actors will now be pariahs in the civilized world.

—TREASURY SECRETARY PAUL O'NEILL, *January 9, 2002* [1]

We will continue to work with our coalition partners to search out terrorists, smash their weapons, smash their networks, and freeze their finances. There will be no respite, no rest until terrorists and terrorism are defeated. And they will be defeated.

—SECRETARY OF STATE COLIN POWELL *in an address on June 14,*
2003, remarks to the annual American-Arab Anti-Discrimination
Committee's National Convention Banquet, Washington, D.C. [2]

We make no distinction between those who carry out terrorist attacks and those who knowingly finance, manage, and supervise terrorist organizations.

—ATTORNEY GENERAL JOHN ASHCROFT, *regarding the indictment of Sami Al-Arian* [3]

S trong words, from the highest level of the Bush administration, have suggested that terrorist money is flowing like rivers, rushing down from terrorist tributaries known to the public as Muslim charitable and educational organizations. On September 23, 2001, President George W. Bush signed Executive Order 13224, authorizing the secretaries of state and treasury to identify, designate, and freeze the U.S.-based assets of alleged terrorists and their supporters. That order provided the authority for an effort unprecedented in history to identify and freeze the assets of individuals and entities associated with Islamic charitable and educational organizations that the government suggested were more fronts for terrorist financing. In announcing the executive action and the freezing of the assets of twenty-seven entities, Bush said, "The message is this: those who do business with terror will do no business with the United States or anywhere else the United States can reach." [4]

The government said it was stopping the flow of terrorist support; the charities, many of which saw their directors arrested or deported, claimed that they were framed by a "guilt by association" mentality that gripped the government post–September 11. In this atmosphere, all things Islamic—at least in this country—were suspect.

Islamic charities and their principals believe that they are being targeted for their political beliefs and for supporting causes inconsistent with U.S. foreign policy. Several cases, before and after September 11, have challenged the constitutionality of the "aiding and abetting terrorism" concept, mostly on First Amendment grounds, with mixed results.

While the First Amendment does not specifically mention the right of association, the accepted right to associate with like-minded people grew out of the amendment's guarantee of the right to peaceably assemble and petition the government. In order to petition the government effectively, one might join others who have the same grievances. This liberty, then, was conceived to protect an association of people formed to achieve some lawful political end. Some commentators consider the right of association a penumbra (a right guaranteed by implication) of the First Amendment that protects the privacy of certain kinds of organizational memberships. Other commentators recognize "freedom of association" as a natural right and thereby a fundamental one, and they believe the freedom of association protects one's membership in any organization that is not involved in criminal activity. Associational rights were heavily litigated throughout the 1940s and '50s, usually involving a person's membership in the Communist Party or in organizations considered subversive to the national interest. For a time, these memberships were punished by the government. Civil libertarians say that we are revisiting those days in today's attack on Islamic charities.

The Legal Underpinnings

The authority for raiding and shutting down Islamic charities came not just from Bush's executive order, but from provisions of the USA Patriot Act, enacted about one month after the Bush order, and from a little-known law first used against so-called terrorist organizations during the Clinton administration (see below). Under the Patriot Act, law enforcement officials were given increased powers to conduct surveillance on nonprofit organizations (or anyone else, for that matter) and to freeze their assets. Here is how the laws work.

FREEZING ASSETS

The International Emergency Economic Powers Act (IEEPA), passed in 1977, was designed to authorize economic sanctions on foreign powers during times of war and national emergency.[5] As such, it was a relatively uncontroversial law, and one that was recognized as an important and legitimate national security policy. During the Cold War, the act was first used to target organizations that supported "communist" causes. Once listed as supporting communism, the organizations and people associated with them were subject to surveillance and investigation. Under the law, placement of an organization on this list is at the will and wish of the president of the United States. An organization can challenge its placement on the list in a federal court, but judicial review is limited. The government does not have to disclose to the organization or the public the precise facts upon which the designation is made, but the reasons supposedly must satisfy a federal judge. (There is also a list of banned organizations kept by the U.S. Treasury Department. The lists are not necessarily duplicative.) President Bill Clinton first used the law in 1995 to ban all government and individual contact with twelve organizations believed to be behind terrorist acts against U.S. interests abroad.

President Bush reached beyond the listing of political organizations to ban charitable organizations that he suggested were fronts for supporting terrorism. Once designated a terrorist organization by the president and placed on the terrorist list, a provision of the USA Patriot Act gives the Treasury Department virtually unlimited powers to shut down offices, seize files and records, and freeze bank accounts, pending what is called an investigation. The determination to freeze assets is made in secret, with secret evidence, and without the ability of the organization or person to challenge placement on the list. Actions against the organizations do not require that there be any criminal activity on the part of the organization. Indeed, though there have been minor criminal violations lodged against individuals involved in the organizations, not one organization or principal has been convicted of a terrorism-related charge to date. Legal challenges to the executive order, to the use of the IEEPA against individuals and organizations, and to the freezing of assets without due process have been unilaterally rejected by all courts that have heard the challenges to date.

What happens to the money the federal government has frozen? It is not going to "terrorists" (if indeed it ever was) and it is not going to legitimate charities. The government cannot actually seize the money, until an organization is convicted of a crime. That would mean the government would have to prove its allegations against the charities. Until now the government has not pushed its cases this far, content to make grand announcements to the press. Having assets frozen means that the charities must apply to the government for any money they need to keep operating. In a legal loophole that must cause great pain to the government, the charities can use their money for legal fees, and the fees are running into the millions of dollars, as lawyers vigorously contest every government action against their clients.[6] Yet the defense has not been successful in freeing these assets.

"MATERIAL SUPPORT" TO TERRORISM

Often the government alleges that the organizations or principals are providing material aid and support to terrorists (e.g., Osama bin Laden), terrorist organizations (e.g., al Qaeda, Hamas, and Hezbollah), or terrorist states (e.g., Syria and North Korea). Section 805 of the USA Patriot Act expands the definition of "material aid and support" to terrorism to include "monetary instruments" and "expert advice or assistance," amending a law passed following the Oklahoma City bombing (the Antiterrorism and Effective Death Penalty Act of 1996; see chapter 1). This part of the statute has had mixed reviews from the courts—and with good reason. It is quite broad. "Material support" can mean the provision of any of the following to an organization or individual the administration labels as terrorist: financial services, lodging, training, expert advice or assistance, false documentation or identification, communications equipment, facilities, weapons, lethal substances, explosives, personnel, transportation, and other physical assets, except medicine or religious materials (Sec. 2339B, Title 18, U.S.C.). There is no requirement that the aid be in connection with a criminal enterprise of the terrorist organization—it could be a wholly peaceful act, such as contributing books for a literacy program operated by a banned organization. Nor is there any requirement that an individual or organization intended to give aid to a terrorist group. The government contends that the statute does not require intent. Quite simply, the charities and their principals are guilty by association. David Cole has written, "The reason material support laws have proven so popular with federal prosecutors is that . . . these laws do not require proof that an individual intended to further any terrorist activity." [7]

In December 2003 the Court of Appeals for the Ninth Circuit ruled that the material support statute was unconstitutionally vague. The case, *Humanitarian Law Project et al. v. John Ashcroft*, involved a challenge to the statute by a human rights organization in Los Angeles and several groups of Sri Lankan Tamils.[8] Reaffirming an earlier decision in the case, the court of appeals held that the statute's prohibition on the provision of "personnel" and "training" to terrorist organizations was unconstitutionally vague.[9] In addition, the court firmly rejected the government's broad interpretation of the "material support" statute. The government argued that the statute permitted a conviction even when a donor was unaware that a recipient organization was designated as a terrorist group and was unaware of the organization's unlawful acts. The court held that this interpretation would unconstitutionally punish "moral innocents" in violation of due process, and it therefore interpreted the statute to require the government to prove beyond a reasonable doubt that the donor knew the organization was designated as a terrorist group or was aware of the unlawful activities that led to its designation.

The court reasoned:

> Without the knowledge requirement described above, a person who simply sends a check to a school or orphanage in Tamil Eelam run by the LTTE [Liberation Tigers of Tamil Eelam] could be convicted under the statute, even if that individual is not aware of the LTTE's designation or of any unlawful activities undertaken by the LTTE. Or, according to the government's interpretation of §2339B, a woman who buys cookies from a bake sale outside of her grocery store to support displaced Kurdish refugees to find new homes could be held liable so long as the bake sale had a sign that said that the sale was sponsored by the Kurdistan Workers' Party (PKK), without regard to her knowledge of the PKK's designation or other activities. [10]

The court also upheld prior rulings that the material support statute's prohibitions on the provision of "personnel" and "training" were "void for vagueness under the First and Fifth Amendments because they bring within their ambit constitutionally protected speech and advocacy."

David Cole, who argued the case, summarized its importance, noting that the administration's interpretation of the statute has a chilling effect on people and organizations that seek to provide humanitarian aid to conflict-ridden areas. More important, he noted, is that the statute imposes guilt by association: "People should be held responsible for their own acts, and for any acts of terrorism that they support, not for their mere 'support' of a group the government has placed on a blacklist." [11]

At the time this book went to press, the Bush administration was appealing the ruling, and ultimately the U.S. Supreme Court will likely decide the fate of the statute under which so many terrorist prosecutions have taken place.

Raids, Closures, and Arrests

Actions against Islamic charities began late in 2001, with a series of government raids on offices, seizures of documents, and arrests of officers. As with the prosecutions against individuals examined in chapter 2, Attorney General John Ashcroft, Federal Bureau of Investigation (FBI) Director Robert Mueller, and prosecutors have made grand public statements about the guilt of those being prosecuted. But to date, not one organization has been charged with *any* crime. Rather, their assets are frozen and their offices shut down. They simply cannot conduct any business or accept any donations. Individuals likewise associated with the charities have not been charged with terrorism, but more often with minor visa violations.

HOLY LAND FOUNDATION FOR RELIEF AND DEVELOPMENT

Terrorist moneymen should know this: We are hunting down the murderers you support, and we will hunt you down. Just as we will prosecute the terrorist who plants a bomb, we will prosecute the terrorist supporter who writes a check. We will follow the money of terror. And we will pursue the financiers of terror as aggressively as we pursue the thugs who do their dirty work.

—ATTORNEY GENERAL ASHCROFT, remarks on the indictment of four brothers involved in a Texas-based Islamic charity, Holy Land Foundation for Relief and Development [12]

The Bush administration took an aggressive stance toward Islamic nonprofit organizations. The first dramatic gesture took place in Bush's home state of Texas, where, on December 4, 2001, the FBI, acting on Bush's order, raided the office of the Holy Land Foundation for Relief and Development (HLF). During a public appearance with Israeli Prime Minister Ariel Sharon, the president said HLF was diverting funds to Hamas, which he described as "one of the deadliest terror organizations in the world today," and providing funds to families of suicide bombers.[13] In announcing the raid, Attorney General Ashcroft rationalized that the government was not just going after those tied to September 11. "With this action we go beyond the al Qaeda network to target groups whose violent actions are designed to destroy the Middle East peace process," he said.[14] The organization was not charged with any crime—it was merely shut down because of government allegations against it.

The shutdown of HLF was a sign that the United States policy toward terrorism financing would target organizations that opposed Israel and other United States allies such as Turkey, India, and Russia. Many of these organizations supported unpopular or resistance causes. Any aid found going to opponents of our allies, or to dissident voices, would be construed as supporting terrorism—regardless of whether any proof existed that it was in fact supporting terrorism.

In shutting down HLF, the FBI followed what quickly became a standard procedure—seizing property and documents, freezing bank accounts, shutting down offices, and arresting principals. In the HLF action, the FBI seized more than five million dollars, along with all documents and property in satellite offices in three states. FBI agents and local police guarded the offices while all property was removed. In *Holy Land Foundation for Relief and Development v. Ashcroft*, the D.C. Circuit Court of Appeals upheld the Office of Foreign Assets Control's designation of the HLF as a "specially designated global terrorist." The court found that there was "ample

evidence" that the foundation had been involved in various meetings with Hamas leaders, had provided funds for Hamas-controlled
charitable organizations, and had financially supported families of
Hamas martyrs. The circuit court upheld the district court, noting
that "there is no free exercise right to fund terrorists." [15] It is important to remember, however, that the HLF had no opportunity to
challenge these allegations or the government's evidence. Indeed,
the government does not even have to disclose its evidence. The
court relies on conclusory affidavits of bureaucrats. Much as enemy
combatants have not been able to challenge the basis for their detention, Islamic charities cannot challenge the basis of their designation as terrorist supporters.

Two weeks after being shut down, Ghassan Elashi, HLF's
founder and cochair, and three of his brothers were arrested on a
thirty-three-count indictment, which indicated no direct ties to
terrorism. The brothers were charged with selling computers and
computer parts to Libya and Syria, both at the time U.S.-designated
"state" sponsors of terrorism. The trial was set to begin in March
2004. No update on these cases is currently available. In announcing the indictment, Ashcroft overstated the case, to say the least,
charging that the HLF was actually a "front" for Hamas, "the most
lethal of Palestinian terrorist groups." Several high-profile Texas
attorneys are defending the brothers. The defense team assailed the
government's mischaracterization of the charges against their
clients. The trading violations allegedly involve selling obsolete
computer equipment. The lawyers charged the Justice Department
with fostering a presumption of guilt because their clients were
Muslims.

GLOBAL RELIEF FOUNDATION

Within days after closing HLF in December 2001, the FBI raided
the headquarters of the Global Relief Foundation (GRF)'s in Chicago, freezing all of its assets "pending an investigation" and tak-

ing computers, filing cabinets, furniture, pictures, and more. On the same day, the Immigration and Naturalization Service (now called the Bureau of Citizenship and Immigration Services) arrested GRF's director, Rabih Haddad, and raided his home. Ultimately, Haddad paid dearly for his association with GRF.

The government's prosecution of Haddad took place entirely in secret, as have many post–September 11 prosecutions. As we have seen, if the government convinces a judge (and this seems easy to do) that national security will be at risk if the proceedings are opened, then judges close the doors and place gag orders on prosecutors and defense attorneys. In the case of immigration proceedings such as the one involving Haddad, Attorney General Ashcroft, by an executive order entered shortly after September 11, began to designate which deportation proceedings should be held in secret (see chapter 5). The Haddad proceedings were not listed on court docket sheets, and the hearings were closed to the press and the public. (Haddad successfully challenged the secrecy of his deportation hearings.[16]) The formal charge that led to Haddad's and his family's deportation was overstaying their visas, but the government originally sought to make a case that the charity was funneling support to al Qaeda, a connection that was never established. Efforts by the American Civil Liberties Union (ACLU) and Representative John Conyers (D-MI) to negotiate with the government and gain political asylum for Haddad and his family were futile. Haddad was arrested just days after federal agents raided the charity's main offices. In July 2003 Haddad was deported to Lebanon without notice to his family. But two weeks later, his wife and four children (ages five to thirteen) were also deported to Lebanon. In November 2003 the U.S. Supreme Court refused to grant appeals to GRF, which wanted to challenge the government's listing of it as a terrorist organization. The Court's refusal to hear the appeal let stand the lower court's rulings that an organization so designated has no right to challenge the designation or to know the basis for the government's case against it.

BENEVOLENCE INTERNATIONAL FOUNDATION

On the same day as the Global Relief Foundation raid, the FBI swooped down on the headquarters of Benevolence International Foundation (BIF), another Islamic nonprofit based in Illinois. On October 9, 2002, Enaam Arnaout, BIF's chief executive officer, a Syrian-born U.S. citizen, was indicted on racketeering charges for misleading donors and using funds to provide material support to terrorist organizations, including al Qaeda. Indeed, the FBI originally alleged that Arnaout had direct ties to Osama bin Laden, charges that were never shown to have any truth. The racketeering charge (which sounds like some Mafia-related offense) was based on statements that the money was going to charitable causes, when it was in fact being used to buy blankets and boots for fighters in Chechnya and Bosnia. Are blankets and boots to be construed as tools of terrorism? Apparently so, if their users are fighting U.S. allies. In announcing the indictment, Ashcroft characterized the charge in terms of good versus evil. "It is sinister to prey on good hearts to fund the works of evil," he said.[17]

With Arnaout's prosecution, the government's policy of shutting down aid to causes that were antithetical to U.S. foreign policy and that of its allies was clear. The government called such support terrorism. The crime actually was that money may have ultimately been reaching organizations on the State Department or Treasury Department's list of banned organizations. The government need not have any proof of this, but in an era of preventive prosecution, its allegations that the money "may be" reaching the hands of terrorists was enough to warrant indictment.

The administration's targeting of Islamic charities may be making political hay at home, but it has a devastating effect on foreign recipients, such as Bosnia, of the charities' largesse. As reported by Andrew Purves in a July 1, 2002, article from *Time Europe*, Lieutenant General John Sylvester, commander of NATO peacekeeping forces in Bosnia, told an audience in Sarajevo, "The irony is that Islamic charities have also done a great deal of good, funneling hundreds of millions of dollars in aid into the Bosnian economy since 1991, supporting everything from mosques to war orphans' education. Already the probe has triggered angry rebuttals from Muslim ambassadors and aid groups who say investigators are casting too wide a net. The deputy director of Bosnia's antiterrorism commission quit because he said his government was focusing too much on Muslims and not enough on known war criminals such as Bosnian Serb leader Radovan Karadzic." [18]

Arnaout's prosecution took many twists and turns. He filed a suit to unfreeze BIF's assets, and in his sworn complaint he said that BIF was not aiding terrorism. Since the government said he was indeed aiding terrorism, they charged him with lying—because he disagreed with them. Ultimately, the judge ruled that he could not be charged with perjury for denying a government charge. If the judge had ruled otherwise, any defendant could be prosecuted for proclaiming innocence, and the presumption of innocence is—or used to be—a cornerstone of individual rights in the United States.

After several charges had not managed to stick to Arnaout, in February 2003 he pleaded guilty to fraud for not disclosing to charitable donors that some proceeds went to buy blankets and boots for soldiers in Bosnia and Chechnya.[19] One has to ask, though, if a U.S. charity would be held to a similar standard. For instance, the Red Cross admitted that it used contributions earmarked for September 11 to fund its general operations, thus misleading the donors. Yet none of its directors was prosecuted for racketeering—or any other crime, for that matter. In August 2003 Arnaout was sentenced to eleven years in prison. Prosecutors had sought a twenty-year sentence, but Judge Suzanne B. Conlon said they had "failed to connect the dots" to prove that Arnaout had al Qaeda connections.[20] It was conceded that he had contact with Osama bin Laden during the Afghan war against the Soviet Union during the

1980s, but the FBI could not establish subsequent contact. Arnaout would not be the first—nor the last—person targeted for prosecution because of his association with a political group that was unpopular with the U.S. government. Prosecutors were taking a page from Cold War–era McCarthyism.

SAA/SAAR

In March 2002 customs agents raided the headquarters of the SAAR Foundation, a cluster of more than one hundred prominent Islamic groups funded mostly by wealthy Saudi citizens with offices in Herndon, Virginia.[21] Several SAAR founders had close ties to the Bush administration and the Republican Party. The organizations and individuals housed there included what the *Washington Post* called some of the nation's "most respected Muslim leaders," including members of the Institute for Islamic Thought and the Graduate School of Islamic and Social Sciences.[22] The purpose of the SAAR investigation, according to the Department of Justice, was to find evidence of money laundering that may be funding terrorist activities. In August the government filed an affidavit claiming the charities gave $3.7 million to BMI, Inc., an investment company the government said may have passed money on to terrorists. Soliman Biheiri founded BMI, Inc., an investment firm that adhered to Islamic principles, in Secaucus, New Jersey, in 1986. (Islamic principles do not condone the payment of interest as such on investments, but require that capital appreciation be tied to business decisions and growth.) In a government affidavit, investigators alleged that BMI attracted millions of dollars in investment capital from the Virginia-based charities, which are largely funded by the Saudi government and wealthy Saudi businessmen.[23]

Prosecutors charged Biheiri not with any act of terrorism, but with "lying under oath" on a 1999 visa application and on his application for U.S. citizenship by failing to reveal all of his foreign travels and employment history. On October 9, 2003, he was convicted by an Alexandria, Virginia, federal jury. The maximum penalty for the offense was six months in jail. At his January 2004 sentencing hearing, the prosecutors requested ten years in prison, asking U.S. District Judge T. S. Ellis III to use a federal guideline that allows stricter punishment if a crime is "intended to promote terrorism." But Biheiri had never been charged with any act of terrorism. So how could he be sentenced under a terrorism law? Prosecutors said that he had "done business" with people "designated" as terrorists by the U.S. government, including people involved with Hamas.[24] Judge Ellis refused to buy that argument. He said that it was not a crime to have social connections with people the government has labeled as terrorists. Further, Ellis said that the government had not proven any connection between Biheiri and terrorist funding. Ellis sentenced him to one year in prison, enhancing the sentence somewhat beyond the maximum of six months. Biheiri was also required to forfeit his citizenship and return to Egypt after he served his sentence. Ellis told Biheiri that he should be grateful that he lived in a country where the law protected him.[25]

The government filed charges against other individuals involved in other Islamic charities not connected with SAAR. In October 2003 an Alexandria, Virginia, grand jury indicted Abdurahman Alamoudi, leader of the American Muslim Foundation, for illegally doing business with Libya, which at the time was on the U.S. government's list of state sponsors of terorrism. He was also charged with money laundering, failing to report travel to Libya, and lying on his application for naturalization years earlier (misstating the number of times he had been out of the country and not listing his connections to his own charity organization).[26] Libya was on the State Department's list of state sponsors of terrorism until early in 2004, when Libyan president Muammar Qadaffi admitted the role of his government in 1986 bombing of an airliner over Lockerbie, Scotland. The September indictment charged that Libya gave

Alamoudi the money to fund Islamic activist groups in the United States. Alamoudi's indictment was all the more ironic inasmuch as he met at the White House with President Bush's senior adviser, Karl Rove, in June 2001 to discuss funding for "faith-based" initiatives.[27] Coincidentally, Alamoudi has close ties to several people high up in the Bush administration. In fact, Alamoudi was largely responsible for the training of Muslim chaplains for the U.S. armed forces.[28]

Alamoudi was said by people close to him to be a moderate Muslim activist and to have some responsibility for improved United States–Libya relationships. However, his downfall may be that at one time he was a vocal supporter of Hamas and Hezbollah, Middle Eastern organizations designated as terrorist groups by the U.S. government and, of course, archenemies of Israel. In December 2003 Alamoudi charged that the prosecutors took his former statements about these organizations out of context.[29] While he may have supported their fight for the Palestinian people, he never condoned acts of terror, he said.

Alamoudi's attorney, Stanley Cohen (who has represented many Muslims and Arabs charged since September 11), attacked the government's case against his client. The indictment charged not one count of supporting terrorism; yet the government's affidavit said that Alamoudi had put funds in the hands of terrorist organizations. A closer look at the indictment shows layers of guilt by association—dots with no connections. The affidavit of Homeland Security agent Brett Gentrup said that Alamoudi was in contact with people who had been designated terrorists and that some of his charity's money reached another charity that itself was believed to have given funds to Hamas. Cohen said, "Once again, despite all the government's hyperbolic ravings and trying to link Muslims to al Qaeda, Hamas, and global jihad, at the end of the day, this is an indictment that only alleges violation of a regulatory scheme with Libya."[30]

On October 17, 2003, federal prosecutors released a 101-page affidavit of Homeland Security agent David Kane, who has led the probe of the Herndon groups. In it, Kane alleges that SAAR organizations run the largest terrorism-financing ring in the world. But look closer, as attorney Nancy Luque urges the public to do, and nowhere will you find any proof that there was ever any support of terrorism. For instance, it is said that the charity used banks that financed Bin Laden and al Qaeda. Yet, the bank in question is a huge Arab bank, similar to our Bank of America. (To put this in perspective, imagine if someone was indicted because he or she did business with a bank involved in funding Enron's phony loans.) There is no smoking gun against Alamoudi in Kane's affidavit, but there is a smoking gun that reveals how Kane shot down the presumption of innocence until proven guilty. In the indictment, Kane said, "There appears to be no innocent explanation for the use of layers and layers of transactions between SAAR Group companies and charities other than to throw law enforcement authorized off the trail." [31] It is funny that the same was not said about Enron. The government's excuse for indicting so few Enron executives is that the layers of transactions are so complicated that the Department of Justice and its host of private attorneys can find scant proof of wrongdoing. Scores of examples could be given in which American corporations get away with fraud that does untold harm to untold millions of people, but the presumption of innocence holds for them. Such generosity is not shown to Islamic charities.

HELP THE NEEDY

In February 2003 federal indictments were handed down against men in Syracuse, New York, and Boise, Idaho, alleging that a charity, Help the Needy, was involved in money laundering to benefit terrorism. As is typical, however, none of the men were actually charged with aiding and abetting terrorism. Four Arab men living near Syracuse were accused of conspiring to evade U.S. sanctions against Iraq (before the United States lifted the sanctions when it invaded Iraq in April 2003) by allegedly raising $2.7 million for unnamed individuals in Baghdad through Help the Needy. This charity, the government alleges, is an affiliate of the Islamic Assembly of North America (IANA), which operates out of Ann Arbor, Michigan. IANA is a branch of the Al-Haramain Islamic Foundation, a charity that is the Saudi equivalent of the United Way and has branches all over the world. The funds were placed in banks in New York and then laundered through an account at the Jordan Islamic Bank in Amman before being distributed to unnamed individuals in Baghdad.

Sami Omar al-Hussayen, a thirty-four-year-old Saudi doctoral candidate at the University of Idaho who allegedly receives financial support from the Saudi government, was accused of designing Web sites that "advocate violence against the United States." [32] The indictment against al-Hussayen contends that he supplied expertise to a Web site associated with IANA that expressly advocated suicide attacks and using airliners as weapons. Originally, he was charged with eleven counts of visa fraud and making false statements on documents by misrepresenting to the Immigration and Naturalization Service that he was in this country solely to attend school and by failing to disclose his affiliation with "professional, social, charitable organizations." However, in January 2004 the federal government indicted al-Hussayen on charges that he aided and abetted terrorism by creating Web sites and moderating an e-mail group that allegedly called for "jihad." The indictment alleges that al-Hussayen knew that the material support he provided was to be used in preparation for murder, maiming, kidnapping, and the destruction of property.[33] Prosecutors have an uphill battle in this case because, as we have seen, the Ninth Circuit Federal Court of Appeals (which includes Idaho, where al-Hussayen was indicted) has already ruled that the material support for terrorism law is unconstitutionally vague. (See afterword for updates.)

The Larger Constitutional Issues

Even though the organizations and principals may have done nothing obviously wrong or terror-related, the power of the USA Patriot Act, FISA warrants, and the political climate post–September 11 has allowed the government to shift burden of proof to the organizations. These organizations must prove their innocence even though, in many cases, there is no allegation of specific wrongdoing waged against them, only a suspicion that funds "must be" reaching terrorists. It is difficult, if not impossible, to prove a negative—or the *absence* of wrongdoing. Moreover, they must do this without access to their own documents, computers, records, or other materials that might make their case. By merely suggesting that national security would be threatened if evidence against the organization is made available to it for defense purposes, the government may present all or part of its evidence to the judge outside the presence of the defendants or their attorneys. Thus, the closure of the charities is based on evidence that the organizations will never see, a procedure approved by the federal courts before whom these cases have been brought.

For now, only Islamic organizations have been shut down, but the Patriot Act puts others at risk of investigation as well. Breaking down the wall between intelligence gathering and criminal prosecution makes it possible for the government to conduct secret and wide-ranging surveillance of nonprofit organizations. For instance, if a terrorist suspect repeatedly logs on to an organization's Web site, the organization and other users of its Web site potentially can be investigated, too—without anyone knowing.

Perhaps because of their inability to find a connection to terrorism, in January 2004 the Senate Finance Committee asked the Internal Revenue Service to turn over confidential tax and financial records, including donor lists, of the charities discussed in this chapter and dozens of others, as part of a planned congressional investigation into the alleged ties between the organizations and

terrorist groups. Committee chairman Senator Charles E. Grass-
ley (R-IA) signaled that the committee was prepared to find the terrorist connections that had so far eluded the FBI and federal
prosecutors. Muslim principals and attorneys for the charities
accused the committee of conducting a fishing expedition to support its presumption of guilt. Inasmuch as the assets of the charities subject to prosecution have been frozen and their operations
shut down, there is nothing else that can be done to the charities
themselves except revoke their tax-exempt status. The Council on
American-Islamic Relations suggested a more ominous purpose—
targeting donors for prosecution because of their charitable giving.[34] Whatever the committee's goal, the investigation will likely
further restrict and limit giving to Islamic charitable organizations.

I asked Ashfran Nubani, an attorney who has represented several of the principals of Islamic charities, including Haddad, what
he makes of the wide-ranging investigation of Islamic charities. His
answer? "If you're an Arab in the United States, you don't get any
justice." [35]

From the looks of things, the government wants to shut down
all Islamic charities and charge the officials with any crime at all—
enough to put them behind bars for years and if they are not citizens, deport them after serving time for minor offenses. In the
words of Attorney Joseph Duffy, who represented Arnaout, "The
government is fighting a paranoid war against any Muslim who ever
had any contact, no matter how innocent, with a terrorist, a suspected terrorist, or an acquaintance of a suspected terrorist." [36]

Just how paranoid the government was about Muslims was seen
in its post–September 11 policy toward Arabs and Muslims living in
the United States, as we will see in the next chapter. It locked up
hundreds on mere suspicion, holding some for months incommunicado, deporting them on evidence of minor violations of law (some
that occurred years earlier), and using secret evidence given in secret
trials. The witch hunt was on, and Muslims were the targets.

5

SEIZURES, DETENTIONS, and DEPORTATIONS

We have waged a deliberate campaign of arrest and detention to remove suspected terrorists who violate the law from our streets. Currently, we have brought criminal charges against 110 individuals, of whom 60 are in federal custody. The INS has detained 563 individuals on immigration violations. . . . Since September 11, the Customs Service and Border Patrol have been at their highest state of alert. All vehicles and persons entering the country are subjected to the highest level of scrutiny. . . . Since 1983, the United States government has defined terrorists as those who perpetrate premeditated, politically motivated violence against non-combatant targets. My message to America this morning, then, is this: if you fit this definition of a terrorist, fear the United States, for you will lose your liberty. . . . We have engaged in a deliberate campaign of arrest and detention of lawbreakers. All persons being detained have the right to contact their lawyers and their families. Out of respect for their privacy, and concern for saving lives, we will not publicize the names of those detained.

—ATTORNEY GENERAL JOHN ASHCROFT, *testimony before Senate Judiciary Committee, December 6, 2001* [1]

In my experience, when the government uses the immigration process to target a "terrorist," one can be fairly certain that it does not have evidence that the individual has actually engaged in or supported any terrorist act. In every case in which I have been involved, the government has loosely invoked the label of "terrorism" but has never even alleged, much less proven, that any of the individuals I represented engaged in or supported any terrorist activity. If it had evidence of such conduct, the government would not be satisfied to send the person abroad, where he would be free to plan and carry out further terrorist acts.

—GEORGETOWN UNIVERSITY LAW PROFESSOR DAVID COLE [2]

According to Attorney General John Ashcroft, as quoted above, and in virtually every press conference and public appearance since that time, the Department of Justice, the Federal Bureau of Investigation (FBI), and immigration authorities have been, since September 11, 2001, rounding up, arresting, charging, convicting, and imprisoning an awful lot of terrorists. Indeed, the months immediately after September 11 will go down in history as dark days in the country's treatment of Arab-American and Muslim citizens and aliens. Laws were passed, Muslims and Arabs were rounded up, and an atmosphere of near hysteria prevailed. There are hundreds, even thousands, of horror stories of innocent people who were questioned or detained because of the color of their skin, their clothing, their last name, or their country of origin.

Yet, as law professor and attorney David Cole aptly notes, not one person detained or deported in those months after September 11 was found to have engaged in a single act of terrorism. Most had just not been entirely truthful on their visa applications. In fact, as one attorney for many of those charged said to me, if any of us were asked to account for every yes or no answer on every government document we filed in our lifetime, we could be prosecuted for government fraud, too. But we are not. If you are an Arab or Muslim here on a visa or with permanent resident status, the government

is looking for a reason to charge you with a crime. And being convicted of fraud, besides being easy to prove, means deportation is
almost certain. As Cole pointed out, had the deported immigrants
engaged in any act remotely tied to terrorism, they would not have
been deported after secret trials. They would have been pilloried
in public, with Ashcroft taking all the credit for nabbing them. Take
the case of a professor, Palestinian Mazen Al-Najjar. He had been
arrested in 1997 for overstaying his visa and was imprisoned for two
years, until November 2000. Why imprisoned? Because there was
no place to deport him. He had no country. But after September
11, 2001, he was arrested again, held in prison until August 2002,
and deported to Jordan, which agreed to accept him. All told, he
spent three-and-one-half years in prison. He was never charged
with a crime.[3]

A similar fate befell Benamar Benatta, an Algerian man who was
arrested by Canadian authorities in Niagara Falls, New York, on
September 11, 2001. Benatta had come to the United States on official business for the Algerian air force. He and other Algerian air
force technicians had been invited to take part in a training program
at the Northrop Grumman Corporation facility. On September 12
he was turned over to U.S. authorities, becoming one of the hundreds detained for questioning for possible connections to the terrorist attacks of September 11. He was held in solitary confinement
in a New York jail, isolated for twenty-three hours a day, and repeatedly questioned about his knowledge of the September 11 attacks.
When the government could not blame September 11 on him, it
continued to hold him in the New York facility until April 2002.
Then, prosecutors brought federal charges against him, accusing
him of having "false documents" in his possession when he was
detained in Canada. He was moved to a federal detention center in
Batavia, New York. On October 10, 2003, federal prosecutors
decided to drop the charges against Benatta when Federal Magis-
trate Judge H. Kenneth Schroeder accused the government of
engaging in a "sham" and illegally holding Benatta under conditions

that were "harsh" and "oppressive." If convicted of the charges, Benatta would have received a few months in jail, at most. But in spite of the dismissal of the criminal charges, there is no happy ending. The government is planning to deport Benatta for overstaying his visa.[4]

It would be impossible to chronicle the stories of all of the Muslim and Arab men who have been detained for months, even years, tried in front of immigration judges in secret, and deported or held for deportation. Putting aside the minor violations for which they were accused, the most troubling aspects of their treatment are how their civil rights were violated in the contexts of their detentions and secret trials, as well as how stereotyping and discrimination led to their being arrested in the first place.

The Legal Basis for Detentions and Deportations

The 1996 Antiterrorism and Effective Death Penalty Act (see chapter 1) created tougher deportation policies for aliens. People overstaying their visas (and thus "illegal" or "out of status") could be more easily deported; people legally here and convicted of certain crimes were automatically deportable; and judicial review of immigration officials' determinations was sharply curtailed. With September 11 came the perception by many in the Bush administration and the American public that Muslims and Arabs were to blame. People were requested to report suspicious activities and individuals. The FBI asked local law enforcement to call on Arabs and Muslims in their communities and see if they would talk willingly about their friends and neighbors. Some law enforcement organizations refused to do so, citing lack of manpower and the desire not to interfere with good relations they had with these communities. Shortly after September 11, males from mostly Arab and Muslim countries were required to report to immigration offices for so-called registration. They were fingerprinted, separated from their attorneys, and their records were searched. If any of their immigration papers were not in order, the men were detained for deportation hearings, many in secret. Many were charged with being connected with terrorism or with having something to do with September 11. None were convicted. Most were deported for minor visa violations, some of which took place years earlier. Others were found to have been convicted of a crime since they entered the United States, crimes that were now deportable offenses. Convictions for which people can be deported range from possessing banned substances to writing a bad check to committing a violent crime. These people were detained until their hearings, after which most were deported. Most of the deportations took place without notice to families. Frantic loved ones reported calling local detention facilities only to find out that their husbands or fathers had disappeared. In many cases, the deportees were moved all over the country from jail to jail, seemingly without reason.

There was nothing illegal in what the government was doing. But the law was applied in a discriminate manner to Arabs and Muslims—Italian and Brazilian aliens, for example, were not made to report, nor were their records searched for abnormalities that would warrant deportation. In late 2003 the administration abandoned the registration requirement, perhaps because the practice did more harm than good. It created distrust of the government among Muslims, and it turned up not one terrorist.

The Inspector General's Report [5]

While noting that law enforcement officials were under extreme pressure after the September 11 attacks, the report of Justice Department inspector general Glenn A. Fine issued on June 2, 2003, details numerous instances of abuse, including situations in which detainees were held too long without being informed of charges against them, were prevented from meeting with family and counsel, and were subjected to unduly harsh treatment. Fine's Office of the Inspector General (OIG) conducted interviews with 762 of the 1,200 detainees who were arrested and charged with visa violations. None were charged with any crimes or acts of terrorism. The OIG also reviewed the detainees' files and the policies and procedures surrounding their detention. The detainees were almost exclusively Muslim men, the majority of whom were from Pakistan.

The OIG conducted the investigation and wrote the report pursuant to Section 1001 of the USA Patriot Act. That section directs the OIG to receive and review claims of civil rights violations by the Justice Department and to inform Congress of its results. The OIG is the only entity other than prosecutors that knows the identity of the detainees. (Ashcroft had ordered that the names of the people arrested be kept secret.)

The report described how immediately after the September 11 attacks, the FBI took the lead in a massive investigation that it dubbed PENTTBOM (for Pentagon/Twin Towers Bombing). In an attempt to garner any leads related to the September 11 attacks, the agency deployed four thousand special agents with three thousand support personnel to work on PENTTBOM. Early on, officials realized that, because the hijackers were not U.S. citizens, any investigation would need to include a significant immigration component. The Justice Department policy was to use whatever legal means were available to detain anyone who might be linked to terrorism. According to the policy, if law enforcement agents encountered any non-citizen while pursuing the PENTTBOM investigation and the individual did not have legal status, the individual would be arrested, even if he or she was not a subject of the investigation. Such an individual would then be placed in the category of individuals "of interest" to the FBI. Thus, the report confirms that people were detained who had violated no law.

The report notes that within a week of the attacks, the FBI had received more than ninety-six thousand tips or potential leads from the public. Many of these tips were general in nature and no more substantial than a landlord reporting on the erratic schedule of a tenant who appeared to be Arab. They also included traffic stops during which Middle Eastern–appearing tourists were found to be carrying photographs of the World Trade Center or other New York landmarks. Because of the directive to cast a wide net to prevent any future attacks and the fear that more attacks might be imminent, individuals who had overstayed their visas or had entered the country illegally were arrested and detained under the auspices of the PENTTBOM investigation.

After each arrest, the FBI assessed whether the person arrested was "of interest" to its terrorism investigation. The FBI classified individuals as being "of interest," "of high interest," or "of undetermined interest." The classification determined whether or not the person would be released and when the person would be released. The OIG audit criticized the inconsistent manner in which these assessments were made. The report stated that the FBI should have taken more care to distinguish between individuals whom it actually suspected of being connected to terrorism and those who may only have been guilty of violating an immigration law or were simply encountered through a PENTTBOM lead.

The report found that more than 40 percent of those detained did not receive notice of the charges or pending immigration action against them for days, even months. Prior immigration regulations required that the alien receive notice of actions against him or her within twenty-four hours of arrest. Ashcroft entered an order immediately after the September 11 attacks allowing forty-eight hours to give notice of charge, an extension that was still repeatedly violated, as was made clear by the OIG report.

With no legal basis, except the powers ordered by Ashcroft, the FBI instituted a policy that these detainees would be held in jails until "cleared" of terrorism or other charges. According to the report, the average length of time that a September 11 detainee was held before he or she was cleared was eighty days. More than a quarter of the clearance investigations took longer than three months. This practice and the Justice Department's "no bond" policy for all post–September 11 detainees were unquestionable violations of even illegal aliens' constitutional rights.

The FBI and Justice Department also violated immigration law. Section 241(a)(1)(A) of the Immigration and Nationality Act requires that non-citizens who have violated immigration law be removed from the United States within ninety days of being issued removal orders. However, the FBI said they could not be removed until it "cleared" them. Thus, even people who agreed to be deported were held for months.

Unconstitutional and illegal detentions were not the only problem the OIG found. There was much to complain about in terms of the way the detainees were treated, especially in the Metropolitan Detention Center (MDC) in Brooklyn and the Passaic County Jail in Patterson, New Jersey. Generally, detainees deemed by the FBI to be of "high interest" to its terrorism investigation were held in high-security facilities such as MDC, where detainees were held under twenty-three-hour lockdown. Detainees deemed to be "of interest" or of "undetermined interest" were held in lower-security facilities such as Passaic. There were numerous allegations of physical and verbal abuse against MDC detainees. Detainees were denied access to family members or attorneys for months at a time. The lights in the cells were continuously illuminated, so that prisoners could not sleep. Numerous reports of serious physical injury were reported to be credible, too. Though the OIG's report stopped short of criticizing Ashcroft, the FBI, or the Department of Justice, to many, the report was a warning of the extent of human and civil rights abuses the Bush administration condoned.

Two days after the report was made public, Ashcroft appeared before the House Judiciary Committee to comment on its findings. Ashcroft said that the actions taken against immigrants post–September 11, "for which we do not apologize," were necessary to protect the United States from another attack. Though the Justice Department, he said, does not condone "abuse," he would do it all again (presumably without the beatings). Indeed, on that day, he announced that the Patriot Act needed to be revised to give him more power to protect the United States.[6] The official response from Justice Department spokesperson Barbara Comstock was, "We make no apologies."

In 2002, before the inspector general's report was filed, the Center for Constitutional Rights (CCR) filed a class action suit against Ashcroft (*Turkman v. Ashcroft*) on behalf of detainees who suffered mental and physical abuse. The allegations in the suit were substantiated by the inspector general's report. The case was pending at the time this book went to press.

Secret Trials

Immediately after September 11, Ashcroft notified chief immigration judge Michael Creppy that he would decide which deportation hearings would take place in secret, based on national security interests. On September 21, 2001, Judge Creppy sent out letters to immigration hearing officers all over the country directing how the secret proceedings were to proceed. Immigration rulings are appealed to U.S. district courts, and the trial judges followed the mandate of the Justice Department and closed the trial court proceedings as well. When the cases got to the district courts, the names of the individuals appeared nowhere on a court docket, the hearings were closed to all family and spectators, and no one involved in the proceedings, including court clerks, were to discuss the cases or even to affirm or deny that any person was being so tried.

Hundreds of aliens who were deported had their cases heard in secret trials. In spite of the efforts of media and civil libertarian organizations to open the hearings, judges who wanted to keep the hearings closed, kept them closed. According to lawyers who represented deportees, some evidence was kept from them and presented to the judge by the prosecutors and immigration authorities. The rationale for keeping the release of evidence from the lawyers and defendants was it was a threat to national security; add to those excuses protection of the defendants' "privacy rights," and you have the Ashcroft justification for secret evidence and secret trials that violate the Fifth (due process) and Sixth (right to fair and impartial trial, right to present and cross-examine witnesses) Amendments to the Constitution. The two federal circuit courts that heard appeals objecting to secret trials ruled in totally opposite ways— the Sixth Circuit Court in Detroit unanimously condemned the secrecy while the Third Circuit in New Jersey let it continue.[7]

The Sixth Circuit case, filed in 2002 by the American Civil Liberties Union (ACLU) and several news organizations including the *Detroit News,* was based on media and public exclusion from the U.S. district court trial of deportation proceedings against Rabih Haddad. Haddad also filed suit in his own name and got a favorable ruling (see chapter 4). In declaring that policy unconstitutional, the United States Court of Appeals for the Sixth Circuit emphasized the value of open proceedings and stressed that any legitimate security concerns must be addressed on a case-by-case basis and not through a categorical closure order. According to the court opinion, "The only safeguard on this extraordinary governmental power is the public, deputizing the press as the guardians of their liberty. . . . The executive branch seeks to take this safeguard away from the public by placing its actions beyond public scrutiny.

Against non-citizens, it seeks the power to secretly deport a class if it unilaterally calls them 'special interest' cases. The executive branch seeks to uproot people's lives, outside the public eye and behind a closed door." [8]

In January 2004 the Supreme Court refused to hear the appeals arising out of these rulings, perhaps signaling that it won't touch some critical cases that determine the very future of our civil rights and judicial systems as we know them. On the other hand, the Court may be showing that it believed the government when it asked the Court not to accept the appeals because it was no longer conducting immigration hearings in secret. The problem with this promise by the government is that there is no way to check its veracity: if hearings were taking place in secret, we, the people, and the press, would have no way of knowing about it.

In cases that were mostly reported in the back pages of national newspapers such as the *Washington Post* and *New York Times*, a pattern emerges in which the Bush administration takes secrecy in court proceedings to new, absurd limits, as the following two cases show. One post–September 11 detainee, Mohamed Kamel Bellahouel, a south Florida waiter of Algerian descent, was detained for questioning after September 11 because he was alleged to have served pizza to one of the September 11 hijackers. Someone also reported that he was seen going to a movie with one of the terrorists. Bellahouel appears to have challenged his detention under a writ of habeas corpus; but since every aspect of this case took place in secret, all records are sealed, and since Bellahouel himself is under a court-imposed gag order, we can only speculate that this was the nature of his case. His petition never appeared on the Miami federal court's trial docket or on the appellate docket of the Eleventh Circuit Court of Appeals. The oral argument in the appeals court was closed to the public and all records sealed. Bellahouel is no longer in custody. Whatever the outcome of the case was, it must not have been satisfactory for Bellahouel, for he filed a petition for review to the U.S. Supreme Court. The Court refused to hear the case.

In October 2003 the U.S. Attorney's Office took secret steps to remove from the public record any trace of a habeas corpus case brought by Adham Amin Hassoun, a Palestinian man from Sunrise, Florida, who was fighting deportation after being labeled a terrorist by an immigration judge late in 2003. The matter is so sensitive that even the government's motion to seal is sealed. Hassoun is the first person in the United States known to have been ordered out of the country for alleged terrorist activities, according to local and national civil rights attorneys, including the director of the ACLU's Immigrants' Rights Project. Hassoun, an activist in south Florida's Muslim community, was arrested in June 2002 by agents from south Florida's Joint Terrorism Task Force, who'd learned of his friendship with alleged "dirty bomber" Jose Padilla (see chapter 2). The two once attended the same mosque in Broward, Florida. Hassoun was accused of overstaying his 1990 nonimmigrant student visa.

In December Hassoun, who is, as of this writing, still incarcerated, filed a twenty-three-page habeas petition in U.S. district court in Miami, Florida. The filing, first reported in the *Miami Daily Business Review*, made public the outline of the government's secret case against him.[9] The petition said the FBI accused Hassoun of recruiting terrorists, taking part in an unidentified assassination plot, and being a member of a group whose leader was convicted in connection with the 1993 bombing of the World Trade Center. U.S. immigration judge Neale S. Foster in Miami also said in court that Hassoun "had contact" with Osama bin Laden, according to the petition. Hassoun and his lawyer deny he's a terrorist. They say the government has produced no evidence to back up its accusations. No one has a clue why the government now wants the case secret.

Prosecution with a Vengeance: The L.A. Eight

For years, law professor David Cole has defended immigrants facing deportation for their political views. But no case better illustrates the Ashcroft Justice Department's policy of justice with a vengeance than that of the so-called L.A. Eight. After seventeen years of failed efforts to deport seven Palestinian men and the Egyptian wife of one of them, the government resurrected its case against two of them. At the time of their initial arrests in 1987, activists Khader Hamide and Michel Shehadeh were allegedly affiliated with the Popular Front for the Liberation of Palestine (PFLP), a Marxist group that has advocated an independent Palestinian state and has been involved in various acts of terrorism. The government alleged that Hamide and Shehadeh helped raise funds for the PFLP in the mid-1980s. Hamide and Shehadeh denied any affiliation with the PFLP and said they were being punished for speaking on behalf of the Palestinian cause. Hamide was a coffee salesman and Shehadeh was a restaurant manager; both lived with their families in California and said they have no connection to terrorism.

In seeking their deportation in 1987, the government relied on a provision of the McCarran-Walter Act, which barred membership in communist groups. But a lawsuit filed by the L.A. Eight led a federal appeals court to declare the law an unconstitutional infringement of free speech, and Congress repealed it in 1990. Even though then-FBI director William Webster admitted in 1987 that none of the men were involved in any terrorist activities and that they would never have been arrested if they had been American citizens, he told the local immigration authorities to proceed with deportation.[10] However, the men won their cases every time and went on to live their lives in the United States. End of story, right?

Not for the Bush administration. In the fall of 2003, immigration authorities said they would again seek to deport Hamide and Shehadeh, under provisions of the USA Patriot Act, for their alleged prior connections to the PFLP, now on the State Department's list of terrorist organizations, for supporting a terrorist group, and for their prior violations of the McCarran Act. Despite the law's repeal in 1990, the provisions remain applicable to Hamide and Shehadeh because the repeal did not apply to cases pending at the time. Yet no one has been prosecuted under the law for more than twenty years. It will be the first case under the provisions of the Patriot Act that allows the deportation of foreign nationals for supporting a "terrorist group."[11] For the purpose of deportation, a terrorist group is defined as two or more persons who have threatened to use or have used a weapon to endanger persons or property. One can think of dozens of lawful uses of a weapon to endanger persons or property—say, in the context of self-defense. So, two Israelis who used guns to shoot Palestinians who were on their doorstep— would that make a terrorist group? Of course not, because the law would not be used against Israelis. But against Palestinians, that is a different story.

Consider the case of former Howard University professor and American citizen of Palestinian descent Abdelhaleem Ashqar. He has been jailed repeatedly for more than five years for refusing to answer grand jury questions. Each time, he goes on a hunger strike and is eventually released. He is not suspected of any criminal activity himself but says the government wants information on Palestinian activists. In October 2003 a Chicago federal judge found him guilty of criminal contempt for refusing to testify before a grand jury, a crime for which he could face several years in prison.[12]

It is hard to avoid the conclusion that these men are being targeted because of their Palestinian heritage at a time when support of Israel is second only to the war on terrorism in the administration's foreign policy agenda. Of the L.A. Eight case, Attorney Cole said,

It's all in the name of the "war on terrorism," the government will say. But the LA 8 case, seen in Arab-American communities as the prime example of U.S. hostility toward Arab immigrants, has probably done more to undermine that effort than any case in the past twenty years. Immigrants from all over the world have come here, distributed magazines discussing the conflicts back home, and sent charitable donations there as well. But the only immigrants in deportation proceedings for doing so for at least a quarter-century have been pro-Palestinian activists.

The vendetta against the L.A. 8 was a critical reason for the Arab community's deep distrust of the government even before 9/11. The cost of that distrust became clear in the aftermath of the attacks, as the government, evidently with no idea where the terrorist threats might lie, rounded up several thousand Arab and Muslim foreign nationals who had nothing to do with terrorism—further alienating the communities it most needs to cultivate. The latest chapter in the L.A. 8 case, courtesy of the Patriot Act, will do nothing to make us more secure—and much to make us less free. [13]

An Iranian Citizen

With Iran dubbed part of the "axis of evil" by President Bush, it is not surprising that Iranian aliens would also be targeted for deportation. As reported by the *Sacramento Bee*, the treatment of Kourosh Gholamshahi is a case in point. He came to the United States eighteen years ago, fleeing persecution in Iran, and forged a new life in Sacramento, living quietly and marrying an American woman. He found odd jobs, including work as a busboy at Denny's and as a security guard for state office buildings. Gholamshahi sought political asylum in 1989 but was denied, and he was ordered deported back to Iran. For years, he continued living in the United States illegally. Before September 11 this was a common occurrence, with the government infrequently following up on such cases unless an immigrant came to the attention of law enforcement. But Gholamshahi's thirteen-year-old deportation order caught up with him in the summer of 2002. With the government newly focused on Middle Eastern men and Ashcroft's post–September 11 declaration that any violation would be used to expel possible terrorists, Gholamshahi found himself shuttled from jail to jail as he awaited his fate, often in cells with convicted violent offenders. After spending almost a year in jail, he was freed on bond pending an appeal of his asylum petition. The likelihood of winning is slim.[14]

A Canadian Citizen

In November 2003 a bizarre story came to light having to do with a Canadian citizen, Maher Arar.[15] In the fall of 2002, Arar was returning from visiting family in Tunisia. He was on his way back to Canada by way of New York City when he was detained at New York's John F. Kennedy International Airport. The reason for his detention: "suspected terrorist." He was flown under U.S. guard to Jordan, where he was handed over to Syrian authorities. He was imprisoned in Syria for more than ten months, in what seems to be the equivalent of the "hole" in U.S. prisons (solitary confinement in total darkness). He says he was repeatedly physically tortured, but Syrian officials deny that their country tortures prisoners. The Syrian ambassador to the United States conceded that Syria took Arar in order to get "information" about Arar's alleged terrorist activities. Ten months of "interrogation" turned up no hint that he was a "terrorist," and he was returned to Canada, against the wishes of the Bush administration. Apparently, Arar's treatment came at the behest of the Central Intelligence Agency (CIA). Anonymous officials of the CIA said that Arar's treatment fit the bill of a covert "extraordinary rendition"—the practice of turning over "low-level, suspected terrorists to foreign intelligence services, some of which are known to torture prisoners," presumably to gain information from the suspects. The practice is so secret that no other details are or ever will be available to the public or Congress. Additional information indicated that "renditions" once took place on U.S. soil, but because the CIA has been loathe to actually physically torture "detainees" since the early 1990s, the CIA and the FBI arrange for the person to be sent to countries that will do the torturing for them. Though many were incredulous at the first news of Arar's capture and detention, later reports revealed that the United States did indeed cooperate with the Canadian government, obtaining information that it turned over to Syrian interrogators. Also, it became known that this was not the first time the United States had facilitated imprisonment of a suspect in a foreign country for interrogation.[16] In January 2004 the Center for Constitutional Rights (CCR), which has been instrumental in litigation challenging government policies since September 11, filed a lawsuit in Arar's behalf, claiming that Arar's deportation to Syria violated U.S. and international laws. Defendants include Ashcroft, FBI director Robert Mueller, and Homeland Security secretary Tom Ridge.

An American Citizen in Saudi Arabia

An American citizen suffered a similar fate and, at the time this book went to press, is still in a Saudi prison. In June 2003 twenty-two-year-old American citizen Ahmed Abu Ali was preparing to return home to Falls Church, Virginia, from Saudi Arabia, where he is a student. However, he was detained by Saudi authorities—at the request of the United States government. The purpose of this "interrogation" was supposedly to discover his involvement in a plot, along with other northern Virginia residents, to provide aid to the rebels in Kashmir who were fighting the Indian takeover of that region. Abu Ali disputes his involvement in the activities of some of his acquaintances, members of the Alexandria Eleven, who were convicted of training to fight against a friend of the United States (India) in an Alexandria, Virginia, federal court (see chapter 2).

We have no way of knowing what, if anything, Abu Ali did that might be illegal under our broad and far-reaching antiterrorist laws. This is beside the point at this time. The point is that an American citizen can't come home, and the U.S. government is working with a foreign country to keep him locked up without a charge, without an attorney, without a trial, and with little hope of returning home.

In a communication with his family, Abu Ali said that he was being threatened with being declared an enemy combatant and shipped to Guantanamo Bay. If this were the case, it would be yet another outrageous act by President Bush—to imprison an American citizen and deny him access to U.S. courts. Attorney Ashraf Nubani has tried in vain to find legal help for Abu Ali in Saudi Arabia. He says no attorney there will touch the case. A conversation with Ali's mother and sister on March 9, 2004, confirmed that Ali was still in Saudi custody, had no access to an attorney, and was, like the prisoners in Guantanamo Bay, Cuba, in a legal black hole.

Abu Ali's case should strike fear in the heart of all Americans and bring to mind Alexander Solzhenitsyn's classic of dissident literature *The Gulag Archipelago.* Is the United States, we might well ask, setting up a worldwide system of gulags to which it will send citizens and non-citizens alike to languish beyond the reach of law? In the report on Abu Ali, the *Washington Post* notes that the United States glibly states that it cannot do anything about him because he is on Saudi soil.[18] Yet the U.S. government put him there so he would be beyond the reach of U.S. law and so that the government would not be accountable for the Saudi's actions.

Unfortunately, the United States is getting quite adept at this alarming tactic. It is using this tactic on a large-scale basis at the U.S. Naval Base at Guantanamo Bay, Cuba.

The Shame of Guantanamo

The shameful treatment of aliens nabbed on American soil is nothing compared to the government's internment of 675 (an approximation, as government figures change from time to time) teenagers and men captured in Afghanistan and Pakistan early in 2002. They are being held without lawyers, without access to families, and without being charged with a crime in Guantanamo Bay Naval Base. They are held, according to Defense Secretary Donald Rumsfeld, whose charge they are under, for intelligence purposes. There are plans to try "some" of them in military tribunals with military lawyers; only civilian lawyers who will work for no pay and agree to a host of government restrictions on their representation and behavior while in Guantanamo will be allowed in the base (see chapter 3). To date, only one or two American lawyers have said they would sign on for a job that could put them in such ethically muddy waters. Guantanamo may also be the site for trials, if there ever are any, of American citizens Yaser Hamdi and Jose Padilla, held as enemy combatants in military brigs on U.S. soil (see chapter 2).

As important as the human issues are, the legal problem inherent in what the U.S. government is doing in Guantanamo is an unprecedented matter for American law. President Bush is the first American president to order people captured on foreign soil—and not fighting for a declared enemy—to be brought to U.S. military prisons and held without being charged, without an attorney, and without access to lawyers or family. American human rights and civil liberties organizations were outraged at such an unprecedented and breathtaking display of presidential authority (see chapter 6). On November 13, 2001, shortly after the U.S. Congress gave President Bush broad wartime powers to fight "terrorism," Bush signed an executive order entitled "Detention, Treatment, and Trial of Certain Non-Citizens in the War Against Terrorism." The order states that any non-citizen can be detained if the president determines that there is reason to believe that the person is or was a member of al Qaeda or has engaged in or supported "terrorism" or "other acts" aimed at injuring the United States.

After the order was signed, U.S. military forces offered bounties to people in Afghanistan and Pakistan in exchange for turning in people they claimed were members of al Qaeda. There seems to have been no rhyme or reason to who was captured, and most intelligence sources say that only a handful of the men could have had any intelligence value. The government contends that since the men are held on Cuban, not U.S. soil, they cannot challenge their detention in U.S. courts. This position is in contradiction of the terms of the lease between the United States and Cuba, which expressly says that the United States has full civil and criminal jurisdiction of all persons and incidents within the forty-five-square-mile area that houses the base, it ignores the fact that the United States prosecutes crimes taking place on the base.

Early on a handful of adult prisoners were released after Secretary of Defense Rumsfeld found that they were of no intelligence value. In 2003 the Defense Department announced that it would be trying some of the men. Deputy Defense Secretary Paul D. Wolfowitz was named the chief overseer of trials and executions—and he would act as an appellate body. The military tribunals would be different from the ones used during World War II to try Nazis. The new rules were created by the Justice Department and the Pentagon to give the government total power over how it would treat and try the men. There would be no judicial review. Wolfowitz would decide any "appeals" and impose sentences, and President Bush would authorize executions. At the time this book went to press, the Pentagon was in the process of revising some of the rules, responding to complaints of military lawyers and judges that the system was profoundly unfair.

The trials at Guantanamo had not taken place at the time this book went to press, for the United States got bogged down in Iraq, and the Pentagon had more pressing concerns. With the release and trials of the prisoners stalled, several human rights and civil liberties organizations joined with private lawyers to challenge the detention of the prisoners. Filing a petition for writ of habeas corpus in the U.S. District Court for the District of Columbia in 2003, the organizations were summarily denied on jurisdictional grounds. In an opinion that was affirmed by the U.S. Court of Appeals for the District of Columbia, the court said that Guantanamo Bay was not a U.S. territory and therefore no one there had access to the federal courts of the United States.

Petitioners appealed to the U.S. Supreme Court. The prisoners who filed the suit (two Britons, since released, two Australians, and twelve Kuwaitis) all claimed innocence, having been in the wrong place at the wrong time and having been identified by unscrupulous sources with no credibility and with one goal—give the United States some names in exchange for monetary reward. The United States admitted that it paid informants in exchange for names of people fighting against U.S. forces. The Bush administration, through its chief attorney, Solicitor General Theodore Olson, urged the U.S. Supreme Court not to take the case. The Court, Olson said, had "no business" dabbling where only the president could go—the conduct of a war. Further, he argued, the 1950 Supreme Court case of *Johnson v. Eisentrager*, in which the court denied twenty-one convicted World War II German war criminals the right to seek habeas corpus reviews of their convictions before military tribunals, was the binding precedent in this case.[19] This is not an accurate analysis. The Eisentrager defendants were charged with crimes and had trials and attorneys. The Guantanamo prisoners have had no such things.

The Court may have recognized this distinction in turning aside the administration's warning to stay away from the case.[20] In November 2003 it granted review of the case, but solely for the purposes of determining if Guantanamo Bay was within federal judicial jurisdiction. The court heard oral arguments on April 20, 2004; a decision is expected in June 2004. If the Court finds jurisdiction, the prisoners will at least have their petitions put on the docket for a hearing. But that does not mean that the Court will decide that the prisoners should be able to see the evidence under which the government has held them or that they should be able to, with attorneys, dispute that evidence and defend themselves. Perhaps bowing to international pressure, especially from allies, the United States began to release some prisoners in February and March 2004. On March 8, five Britons were released to their government's custody. Within two days, they had been interrogated and released. British law enforcement found no cause to detain them.

In an ironic historical footnote, one of the many appeals filed on behalf of the Guantanamo Bay prisoners with the U.S. Supreme Court was submitted by Fred Korematsu, who was himself a litigant before the Supreme Court more than forty years ago in a case that tested the right of the government to intern Japanese Americans living on the West Coast during World War II. Then twenty-two years old, Korematsu refused to turn himself in to be locked up, and he was prosecuted and convicted of defying the court order of internment. The Supreme Court upheld the internment order and the conviction, in one of the sadder decisions in the Court's history. In upcoming cases, the Supreme Court may rely on that decision and its deference to executive power in the time of war. A victim of that deference, Korematsu warned in his brief, "We tend too quickly to sacrifice . . . liberties in the face of over-broad claims of military necessity." He went on to say that courts too often "deferred to exaggerated claims of military necessity and failed to insist that measures curtailing constitutional rights be carefully justified and narrowly tailored." [21] (See afterword for updates.)

What These Detentions Have in Common

The detentions and deportations of immigrants living in the United States and the imprisonment of enemy combatants in Guantanamo (and of American citizens in military prisons) share the same modus operandi: all are based upon the claim that the president and Attorney General Ashcroft can exercise executive privilege and rely on secret evidence, if there is any evidence at all, for detaining and imprisoning people. The immigrants who were deported had some semblance of a hearing and may have had counsel if they were fortunate enough to retain an attorney, but the evidence against them was sometimes not disclosed (some had violated immigrations regulations in the past or engaged in some activity that rendered them deportable); for hundreds, their hearings were in secret. Only the lucky ones were able to challenge their deportation in courts. Most against whom proceedings were undertaken were either deported or are imprisoned waiting to be shipped out. Enemy combatants in Guantanamo, American citizen Abu Ali, and Canadian citizen Arar have had no opportunity for any hearing whatsoever.

The most obvious conclusion to be drawn from these practices, as Cole pointed out, is that the government has weak cases against them that could not withstand judicial scrutiny in any American court. None of the Guantanamo prisoners or Americans have been charged with any crime. They have been variously imprisoned, perhaps tortured, and held without access to lawyers, their families, or the courts. Treating people in this way is so contrary to the American system of justice and to the U.S. Constitution that one wonders why there is not outrage from the American public. Perhaps it is because most of the victims of these policies are not American citizens, and there is a lack of empathy for aliens. This is a huge mistake, however, because in Hamdi, Padilla, and Abu Ali, we see American citizens removed from the rule of law. For a nation that prides itself on being a nation of laws, the detentions of mostly immigrants post–September 11 were a historical low point, politically and legally. More importantly, the United States lost its image of being a protector of civil and human rights. It can no longer insist with moral authority that other countries give its citizens protections under international law when Americans are on foreign soil.

These policies and practices can have no good effect whatsoever; the evil that they do to the rule of law and to America's image
abroad will be felt for generations to come. In the next chapter, we
examine a growing grassroots resistance movement made up of
diverse groups of people and organizations challenging the policies
of the Bush administration.

6

POPULAR RESISTANCE in the WAR on CIVIL LIBERTIES

The Patriot Act is purported to better protect America against terrorism; however, it succeeds in not only taking away the rights of terrorists, but of every American man, woman, and child. . . . [It] has violated the rights and freedoms of every American citizen, and it should not be tolerated. The Libertarian Party of Alabama is looking for people to spearhead a project to let Congress know that these violations of our freedom will not be ignored. We need liberty-minded, freedom-loving individuals who will help in the battle to win back our civil liberties. We will be working with Alabama legislators, city council members, and county commissioners to put forth resolutions against the Patriot Act.

—MIKE RSTER, *Libertarian Party of Alabama* [1]

Seattle's public library printed three thousand bookmarks to alert patrons that the Federal Bureau of Investigation (FBI) could, in the name of national security, seek permission from a secret federal court to inspect their reading and computer records—and prohibit librarians from revealing that a search had taken place. Hillsboro, Oregon, police chief Ron Louie has ordered his officers to refuse to assist any federal terrorism investigations that his department believes violate state law or constitutional rights.[2] Wherever there is war, there is resistance. As we have seen most recently in the war in Iraq, the old order does not so willingly give way to the new conqueror. In the war on civil liberties, resistance was slow to emerge. Maybe that's because the level of hysteria was initially so high that the few who questioned things such as rounding up immigrants or passing new draconian laws were quite openly referred to as traitors. Ashcroft called the doubters "terrorist sympathizers." Well into year two in the war on civil liberties, pockets of resistance began to emerge. Today, their roots have spread all over the United States, among all political parties and ethnic groups. Ashcroft says the resistance is born of "baseless hysteria."[3] If that is the case, this hysteria is growing.

Grassroots Resistance

On October 1, 2003, Chicago, Illinois, became the largest city in the country to take action against the USA Patriot Act. A resolution passed by the city council reaffirmed the rights of citizens under the U.S. Constitution and called for the city to work for the repeal of the Patriot Act and executive orders violative of "our fundamental rights and liberties."[4] The Chicago resolution was remarkable because of how it was initiated. Chicago Arabs and Jews, represented by the Jewish Counsel on Urban Affairs (JCUA) and the Muslim Civil Rights Center (MCRC), joined forces to protest the post–September 11 intrusions into the rights of Muslim and Arab American immigrants and communities. Large numbers of immigrant workers had been arrested on numerous occasions, including in raids at O'Hare and Midway airports as well as at the Sears Tower; these raids also led to the detention and deportation of many Latino immigrant airport workers. Both organizations saw the opportunity to bring their members together to fight for a common goal—protecting civil liberties.[5]

JCUA staff attorney Noah Leavitt explained that the Muslim-Jewish solidarity was born of the Jewish group's understanding of what it means to feel the effects of scapegoating and racial profiling.[6] From the inception of anti-Arab and anti-Muslim bias after September 11, the JCUA issued public statements condemning the vandalism of mosques and other community centers, and it forged links to the Arab American and Muslim communities, working with Chicago's MCRC. Other partners in getting the resolution passed were the Bill of Rights Defense Committee, Amnesty International, and the American Civil Liberties Union (ACLU).

Chicago was one of more than two-hundred-fifty counties and municipalities in twenty-eight states and two entire states—approximately forty-three million people—that have passed resolutions criticizing the Patriot Act. The list includes Los Angeles, New York City, Detroit, San Francisco, St. Petersburg (Florida), Baltimore, and Philadelphia. The day before the Chicago resolution, Montgomery County, Maryland, a large county contiguous to Washington, D.C., passed a similar resolution 8–1. The resolution specifically referred to Section 213 of the law, which permits sneak-and-peek warrants (see chapter 1 for a more thorough discussion); Section 215, which authorizes searches of library, bookstore, business, medical, university, and Internet service provider records without any showing of probable cause that a crime has been committed and which prohibits individuals from disclosing that they have been ordered to produce such letters; and Section 802, which creates the new crime "domestic terrorism," defined so broadly that it could be applied to acts of civil disobedience wholly unrelated to terrorism, such as the antiwar rally at Drake University (see afterword).

Almost as noteworthy as the Montgomery County action was the fact that the *Washington Post*, with scores of reporters on staff to cover local news, did not report the event. And while the *Chicago Sun-Times* reported on the resolution, it referred to it as a "watered-down" version (initially the proposal called for a wholesale condemnation of the Patriot Act; in its final form it called for repeal of portions of the act that erode civil liberties).[7] The press, apparently asleep during the passage of the act, has not been very interested in covering resistance to the act. When they do cover it, they do so in a perfunctory manner.

In order to capitalize on the growing resistance to civil liberties intrusions, in mid-October 2003 a national grassroots organizing convention, known as Grass Roots America Defends the Bill of Rights, sponsored by the Massachusetts-based Bill of Rights Defense Committee, took place in Montgomery County, Maryland. The convention featured seminars on how to organize resistance to the Patriot Act. Conservative and liberals joined forces, with organizations such as the ACLU joining with the Eagle Forum (a right-wing organization headed by Phyllis Schlafly devoted to "traditional" American values and opposed to abortion, feminism, and other "liberal'" agendas), to stop the spread of laws that were anathema to the Bill of Rights. The primary goals of the conference were: (1) to strengthen local organizing by coordinating efforts and fine-tuning the process of passing resolutions; (2) to expand the movement to other entities, such as religious organizations, schools, unions, and professional associations; (3) to provide skills for lobbying federal and state legislatures; and (4) to develop strategies for making civil liberties an issue in the 2004 presidential campaign.

Members from many of the jurisdictions where anti–Patriot Act resolutions had been passed provided tips and training on how to organize and capitalize on growing discomfort with the law. Among them was City Councilor Dave Meserve of Arcata, California, who was instrumental in the passage of an ordinance against the Patriot Act that bans city officials from cooperating with the act, under penalty of a fifty-seven-dollar fine. Meserve told conferees, with reference to the federal assaults on privacy rights and due process: "Our message is simple—not in *our* town, you don't!" Hope Marston, an organizer from Eugene, Oregon, described how the Oregon Bill of Rights Defense Committee recently swept the state senate into passing a resolution, despite reluctance from many of their allies who said they couldn't do it. "The grassroots cannot be stopped," she said, referring to the work that brought many Republicans to vote with Democrats 23–2 for the measure.[8]

Congress Responds to the Resistance Movement with the CLEAR Act

But Congress was not going to sit still while municipalities refused to assist the federal government in enforcing the USA Patriot Act. The proposed CLEAR (Clear Law Enforcement for Criminal Alien Removal, HR 2671) Act would encourage local and state police departments to arrest undocumented immigrants. According to the bill's sponsor in the House, Representative Charlie Norwood (R-GA), nothing in this bill mandates anything from law enforcement. But if a locality decides to enforce immigration laws, it will have access to $2.6 billion in federal funding. If the locality chooses not to, it will not be eligible for the one-billion-dollar grant program created by the bill or for any funding from the State Criminal Alien Assistance Program.[9] Police chiefs and departments across the country oppose the law for reasons ranging from being overworked and understaffed to not wanting to target members of ethnic communities with whom they wish to maintain cooperation and good community relations.[10]

The American Civil Liberties Union and the Center for Constitutional Rights

Two stalwart public interest legal organizations are leading the resistance in the courts: the ACLU and the Center for Constitutional Rights (CCR). Though the ACLU is involved in resistance in significant ways (e.g., it sponsors Web sites through which people can send faxes to congressional representatives), by far its most important role is in the courts. From bringing cases in its own name to filing amici briefs, the ACLU is doing what it does best—defending the Bill of Rights. Membership and donations increased steadily after September 11. In addition to the ACLU's active involvement in the cases of enemy combatants Yaser Hamdi and Jose Padilla (see chapter 2), a sampling of cases in which the ACLU plays an instrumental role, usually assisted by several other public interest organizations such as the CCR, include: [11]

❖ A federal suit in Detroit, Michigan, challenging Section 215 of the USA Patriot Act, which authorized searches of library and other institution records (see above). The ACLU has argued that this change violates constitutional rights. The Justice Department said people's Fourth Amendment rights do not extend to records or personal belongings that they have provided to third parties. The government also said it has never used the provision, a statement inconsistent with Justice Department reports based on press queries about library records that had been seized on about fifty occasions.

❖ A federal suit in Detroit challenging the governmental blanket ban on media and public access (including family members) to immigration hearings of people detained after September 11. A memo from chief immigration judge Michael Creppy (see chapter 5) to all immigration judges required that all deportation proceedings be closed to the public and the press when directed by the Justice Department. On April 3, 2002, Judge Nancy G. Edmunds of the U.S. district court granted the ACLU's motion for a preliminary injunction against the use of the policy in the case of Rabih Haddad. The charges against him were never proven, but Haddad was deported (see chapter 4). On August 26, 2002, the Sixth Circuit Court of Appeals unanimously upheld Edmunds's opinion, one of the few wins for civil libertarians in the administration's war on civil liberties. Judge Damon Keith wrote the unanimous appellate court opinion, in which he said, "Democracies die behind closed doors." [12]

❖ In a federal suit in New Jersey similar to the one filed in Michigan, however, the results were the opposite. After a New Jersey federal district court rejected the government's blanket secrecy policy in favor of one that showed some particular reason why harm would result from having an open hearing, the Third Circuit Court of Appeals reversed this decision. A three-judge and then a full en banc (eleven-judge) panel ruled in favor of the government, saying that judges had to follow the dictates of the Justice Department. The ACLU filed an appeal to the U.S. Supreme Court, but the Court declined to hear the case. However, the government said that it is not "currently" conducting secret hearings and that it may change its policy in the future.

❖ A federal suit in the District of Columbia challenging the federal government's refusal to disclose basic information about individuals arrested and detained since September 11, 2001. Judge Gladys Kessler ordered the government to release the names of detainees and their attorneys but issued a stay of her order after the government appealed. The court of appeals for the District of Columbia reversed Judge Kessler. In January 2004 the U.S. Supreme Court refused to hear the case, thus giving the Bush administration a big win in its efforts to keep secret much of its treatment of immigrants post–September 11.

❖ A suit in New Jersey state court for names of all United States Citizenship and Immigration Services (USCIS, formerly INS) detainees held by immigration authorities in certain jails in New Jersey. The case was pending at the time this book went to press.

❖ A federal lawsuit against the Transportation Security Administration for civil rights violations stemming from the wrongful arrest of a Florida doctor of Indian descent by air marshals in Philadelphia because they "didn't like the way he looked." The case was pending at the time this book went to press.

❖ A request to the FBI under the Freedom of Information Act requesting information about government surveillance of college professors and students post–September 11. The suit stemmed from the fact that the FBI was recruiting campus security and police officers to work under its direction and control. The FBI never responded to the request.

❖ A federal lawsuit in northern California challenging the secret "no fly" and other transportation watch lists. The government has refused to confirm the existence of any protocols, procedures, or guidelines as to how the "no fly" lists were created or to explain how they are being maintained or corrected. Further, there is no mechanism for people who are mistakenly on the list to have their names removed. The ACLU has obtained information that there is at least one other list in addition to the "no fly" list—a "selectee" list that establishes which air passengers are to be singled out for additional searches.

❖ A friend-of-the-court brief in the Second Circuit Federal Court of Appeals concerning the government's abuse of the material witness statute used to detain Osama Awadallah, a Jordanian-born college student charged with making two false statements during a grand jury proceeding. The court ruled that the material witness statute was broad enough to cover grand jury proceedings and found that the length of time that Awadallah was imprisoned was not "unreasonable." The appellate court also reinstated the criminal perjury charge.[13]

❖ Five lawsuits in federal courts in New Jersey, Maryland, and California against American, Continental, Northwest, and United airlines for discrimination in ejecting five men from flights based on alleged prejudices of airline employees and passengers. The litigation was pending at the time this book went to press.

As long as civil liberties are violated, the ACLU will continue to file cases. Its Web site (www.aclu.org) is constantly updated with reports on new and pending cases.

Concern over Guantanamo

Human Rights Watch, Amnesty International, and the American Red Cross have publicly criticized the treatment of the prisoners at Guantanamo Bay (see chapter 5). The International Committee of the Red Cross (ICRC) issued a scathing report in October 2003 about the mental and physical health of the prisoners. Having been imprisoned for more than two years and subject to repeated interrogations (as least that is what the Pentagon says is the rationale for holding them) with no hope of release, many prisoners are reported to have a mental state bordering on hopelessness. There have been reports of several suicide attempts, some of them repeated, and there is no way of knowing how many suicides have been attempted or successful but unreported. The only news that comes out of Guantanamo is what the Pentagon wants released.

Human Rights Watch and Amnesty International are also concerned about the prisoners' mental and physical health, but they are
more focused on the illegality of their detentions. The U.S. government has declared the prisoners to be in an essentially "law-free"
zone (see chapter 5). Being held without charges or trials are violations of the Geneva Convention's regulations regarding the treatment of prisoners of war, but the United States claims that these
people are not prisoners of war, merely "detainees" being held for
intelligence purposes. Both organizations are particularly troubled
by the juveniles detained at Guantanamo, the three youngest of
whom were released in February 2004. The efforts of Amnesty
International and the Red Cross may have affected the Supreme
Court's decision to hear the appeal of some of the detainees (see
chapter 5).

Strange Political Bedfellows in the Resistance Movement

Concern over the erosion of civil liberties is creating some odd
partnerships. The grassroots movement resisting the USA Patriot
Act, for instance, counts as partners the National Rifle Association, the Libertarian Cato Institute, and the liberal organization
People for the American Way.[14] Conservative *New York Times*
op-ed writer William Safire joins outspoken filmmaker (*Bowling
for Columbine*) and author (*Dude, Where's My Country?*) Michael
Moore in condemning the government's encroaching powers over
individuals.[15]

What little resistance there is in the U.S. Congress is biparti-
san. On October 15, 2003, a group of lawmakers and advocacy
groups formed a Coalition of Conscience to roll back sections of
the Patriot Act they say encroach on civil liberties. The SAFE Act
(Security and Freedom Ensured) of 2003 was authored by Senator

Larry E. Craig (R-ID) and Senator Dick Durbin (D-IL). The bill was cosponsored by senators Russell Feingold (D-WI), John Sununu (R-NH), Mike Crapo (R-ID), Jeff Bingaman (D-NM), Ron Wyden (D-OR), and Lisa Murkowski (R-AK). The legislation targets four areas of the Patriot Act: "delayed notice" warrants, wiretaps, surveillance at libraries, and multijurisdiction warrants. The bill would limit the use of sneak-and-peek search warrants to situations in which a life is at stake, evidence may be destroyed, or there is a flight risk. Roving wiretaps, which allow the surveillance of any phone a person is known to use, could only be employed when the suspect is present. Warrants for these wiretaps must also identify the target and location of the wiretap. The bill also reinstates pre–Patriot Act standards for seizing business and library records and requires that the FBI must show why a suspected terrorist or spy is being targeted. Library computers could not be searched without a court order.

Several organizations endorsed the Safe Act, including the Gun Owners of America, Free Congress Foundation, Center for Democracy and Technology, Electronic Frontier Foundation, American Booksellers Foundation for Free Expression, Center for National Security Studies, American Library Association, and the ACLU.[16] In January 2004 Attorney General John Ashcroft promised that President George W. Bush would veto the Safe Act, if and when it passes the Congress. In a letter to senate judiciary committee chairman Orrin Hatch (R-UT), Ashcroft said that the proposed legislation would "undermine our ongoing campaign to detect and prevent catastrophic terrorist attacks."[17]

The sternest rebuke to the administration came in July 2003 when the House voted to cut off money for searches in which the notification is delayed. The sponsor was conservative Representative C. L. "Butch" Otter (R-ID), and his amendment was supported by 112 fellow Republicans who had voted for the original law in 2001. The Senate, however, did not follow suit, and as the 107th

Congress ended their session, debate about what to do about the Patriot Act and other controversial laws was postponed for the new Congress. At the time this book went to press, pundits predicted that no wide-scale changes would be enacted in 2004, an election year. With the more controversial provisions set to expire in 2005, little action to curtail the Patriot Act is expected until after the 2004 election. No hearings have been scheduled on the Safe Act. Further, there may even be efforts to extend the act during the election season, especially if President Bush has his way. In his State of the Union Address in January 2004, Bush called on Congress to extend the Patriot Act provisions that are set to expire. "The terrorist threat will not expire on that schedule. Our law enforcement needs this vital legislation to protect our citizens," he said.[18]

What You Can Do

"That's all well and good," you may say of city counsel resolutions, ACLU lawsuits, and proposed acts of Congress. "But what can I do?" I am amazed by the number of times that I am asked that question in response to a lecture I have given or an article I have written. My first response is, do what I do: write. There are any number of avenues for a literate person to speak his or her mind and to inform others about the dangers to liberty coming from within our government. Local newspapers, community and organizational newsletters, Web logs, church bulletins—all may have space for informational and opinion pieces. You don't have to be a polished writer to share your views with others. Passing along articles by way of e-mail is a fine way to educate even those who may not want the education. I send out dozens of e-mails a day to different people. "Read this," I say. "This is something you might need to be aware of." (See resources for keeping current in the back of this book for up-to-the-minute information.)

Speaking out formally in organization meetings and local political gatherings is another way to educate your friends and neighbors. Making copies of articles and laws and passing them out in your organization or even leaving them lying around in beauty parlors and doctor's waiting rooms is another way of making people aware of threats to liberty. When I recently found an article about an amendment to the USA Patriot Act that creates a sort of presidential secret police, I made copies and had them ready to give to people who don't "do" e-mail.

Joining and making contributions to organizations that are on the front lines of resistance is an easy way to make a difference. At no time in modern history have the ACLU and the CCR been so busy in so many courts. Their human and financial resources are stretched to the limit—but the number of their supporters is growing. It is amazing to me how often I get pleas from readers who wonder if the ACLU will take their case. Well, the ACLU has to have money to take these cases. We want them to be there for us when Ashcroft and Bush are shredding the Bill of Rights, so we had better be there for them.

Then, of course, there is the issue of voting. Granted, there may not seem to be very many candidates to support who are speaking out for civil liberties and against the Patriot Act. After all, the bill was named "Patriot" not just because it made a cute acronym—but rather because to be against it is to be, by the administration's definition, unpatriotic. This view in itself needs vociferous challenge. What self-respecting American is going to stand for the proposition that to question the government is to be a traitor? Yet too many of us have stood for this attack on civil liberties out of fear of being so labeled ourselves.

At the very minimum, all Americans can pay attention to the laws, read credible new sources, and talk about what they read and hear. They can question each other and engage their friends and family members in debate. For four years, Americans have ignored the proverbial elephant in the living room: Ashcroft and his vision of an America guided by a new Constitution of his own writing. President Bush is content to let Ashcroft ride roughshod over our rights and pretend to distance himself. The Congress enables it, the courts barely condemn it, and we, the people, sit and talk about how shameful it is.

The shame lies in selling liberty down the river in the name of fighting a war that can never be won. We had better start resisting in whatever way we can. Too soon, complacency and contentment set in, allowing freedom's captivity by the forces of greed and power, which parade as defenders of national security and protectors of liberty. In the last chapter, we consider if, when, and how this war on civil liberties will end.

7

A WAR WITHOUT END

As we gather tonight, hundreds and thousands of American servicemen and -women are deployed across the world in the war on terror. By bringing hope to the oppressed and delivering justice to the violent, they are making America more secure. The terrorists continue to plot against America and the civilized world. And by our will and courage, this danger will be defeated.

—PRESIDENT GEORGE W. BUSH, *State of the Union Address,* *January 20, 2004* [1]

As we enter the fourth year in the war on terror, it is important to reflect on what it has become—morphing from a plan to retaliate against the perpetrators of September 11, to a justification for the war on Iraq, to a justification for using powers under the USA Patriot and Homeland Security acts to prosecute nonterrorist crimes. In this chapter we explore how President George W. Bush and Attorney General John Ashcroft's war on terror may continue to affect life in the United States in the foreseeable future, in

spite of an inevitable (at some point) change in administrations.
From classifying common criminal offenses as crimes of terror, to
blaming economic woes on the demands of fighting that war, to
demanding more laws to prosecute the war at home, to engaging in
preventive arrests and prosecutions, to making the war on terror
the cornerstone of foreign policy, and to formulating strategies and
schemes we cannot begin to know at this time, the Bush administration has encroached on civil liberties to such a degree that the
America we knew before September 11 is no more.

Terrorism Is a Dangerous Word

According to John Whitbeck, an American citizen who practices
law in Saudi Arabia and France and writes political commentary
published in numerous foreign newspapers, the way the word *terrorism* is being used is fraught with danger. For years, people have
recited the truism, "One man's terrorist is another man's freedom
fighter." However, with the world's sole superpower declaring an
open-ended, worldwide war on terrorism, the notorious subjectiv-
ity of the concept holds frightful possibilities. After all, as we have
seen repeatedly, the word has dozens of meanings in U.S. laws and
regulations alone. The Bush administration bandies it about freely
so as to invoke fear and "terror" in the listener. Says Whitbeck:

> There is no shortage of precise verbal formulations for the diverse
> acts to which the word "terrorism" is often applied. "Mass murder,"
> "assassination," "arson," and "sabotage" are available (to all of
> which the phrase "politically motivated" can be added if appropri-
> ate), and such crimes are already on the statute books, rendering
> specific criminal legislation for "terrorism" unnecessary. However,
> such precise formulations do not carry the overwhelming, demo-
> nizing, and thought-deadening impact of the word "terrorism,"

which is, of course, precisely the charm of the word for its more cynical and unprincipled users and abusers. If someone commits "politically motivated mass murder," people might be curious as to the cause or grievances that inspired such a crime, but no cause or grievance can justify (or even explain) "terrorism," which, all right-thinking people agree, is the ultimate evil. [2]

Since the United States makes so much political hay with the term, it is no surprise that foreign governments have followed suit. Every government facing an insurgency or dissent movement claims that the dissidents are "terrorists," and anyone who questions the government's motives in quelling terrorism become themselves terrorist sympathizers, terrorists, or traitors. Such has been the state of affairs since September 11 in this country. And before that, the Palestinians and Chechnyans were routinely referred to as terrorists. Whitbeck suggests that the only globally workable definition of "terrorism" is subjective—"whatever I do not support."

REDEFINING THE TERM

Georgetown University law professor David Cole similarly notes that the U.S. government defines "terrorism" in various ways depending on the regulation's targeted population or activity. [3] The most stringent definition is used in immigration regulations, [4] and it is currently being employed indiscriminately against Arab and Muslim aliens, which the government justifies because "these types" were involved in September 11. The U.S. government's lists of terrorist organizations and states is likewise selective, omitting Saudi Arabia, the home country of most of the September 11 terrorists, and including Cuba and Syria. An interesting bit of history is attached to these lists. Even though the 1996 Antiterrorism and Effective Death Penalty Act (see chapter 1) authorized the establishment of a terrorist organization list, the list was not activated until after a peace of sorts was achieved in Northern Ireland. Why? Because the government did not want to put the Irish Republican Army (IRA) on the list (the Clinton administration was working on securing peace in Northern Ireland), and it did not want to answer questions about why the Popular Front for the Liberation of Palestine would be on the list (as it was) and not the IRA. Both engaged in violence against civilians, both for political purposes. Israel engages in violence against civilians, but Israel will never be found to be a state sponsor of terrorism. Yet Syria is listed as a terrorist state because it allows organizations such as Hamas and Hezbollah to have offices in Damascus. Is it fair to say that Syria is a terrorist state only because those organizations have members and offices there? When in fall 2003, President Bush referred to travelers to Cuba as supporting the "terrorist" regime of Fidel Castro, he was extending the reach of the term beyond its traditional meaning—violence against civilians in order to effect some political agenda—to include travel to a country the U.S. refuses to engage with. Bush promised that the prosecutors would "target" American citizens who travel to Cuba.

The balkanization of the term *terrorism* undermines the gravity of its threat to global security. Calling every cause, country, or organization antagonistic to U.S. ideas "terrorist" sets up a black/white, "we/they" world that works for President Bush, who said in the days immediately after September 11, "you are either for us or against us and if you are against us, you are a terrorist."[5] The world is too complicated for such a simplistic rubric.

NEW CRIMES OF "TERROR"

In the summer of 2003, prosecutors in North Carolina charged a maker of methamphetamine with terrorism, alleging that methamphetamine is a biochemical weapon of mass destruction, which, according to the law, is "any substance designed or capable of caus-

ing death or serious injury." Prosecutors in Virginia lodged terrorism charges against an adult and juvenile known as the "Beltway
snipers" for their role in killing several people in drive-by shootings in the District of Columbia metropolitan area in the fall of
2002. Calling the shootings crimes of terror made the perpetrators
eligible for the death penalty and played on the emotions of residents of the area who, with a word, became victims of "terrorism."[6]
Federal prosecutors in California charged a man with possession of
a terrorist weapon of mass destruction when a pipe bomb exploded
in his lap. In May 2003 a lovesick twenty-year-old woman from
Orange County, California, aboard a Hawaii-bound cruise ship
with her family was charged with planting threatening notes in
order to make the ship return her to port so she could see her boy-
friend. She was sentenced to two years in federal prison for violating a provision of the Patriot Act that makes it a crime of terror to
make a threat against a mass transportation system. At the time this
book went to press, Attorney General John Ashcroft was promot-
ing passage of new legislation, known as the VICTORY Act, which
would make many existing crimes—from dealing in drugs and
pornography to committing murder—crimes of terror and would
create new criminal laws for terror-related offenses.[7] If successful,
this plan will lead to longer prison terms for existing crimes and
allow for crimes to be prosecuted as acts of terror (such as demon-
strating against the war, as is discussed in the Drake University case
in the afterword.)

No less than avowed Bush supporter G. Gordon Liddy took aim
at the Patriot Act and the proliferation of anti-terror laws. "I find
a trend that is the more odious the proposed law, the more glori-
ous the title. And when they come up with the Mom and Apple Pie
Act I'm really going to say watch out."[8]

Worse than renaming ordinary crimes acts of terror is the use
of the Patriot Act to investigate so-called ordinary crimes. Federal
authorities in Nevada made use of Section 314 of the Patriot Act

to subpoena records related to the bribery of federal officials, racketeering, and the operation of prostitution rings. The Justice
Department sent faxed subpoena requests to financing institutions
seeking banking records of individuals targeted. No court order is
required if the government says it is investigating people suspected
of being involved in "terrorist acts or money laundering activities."
To the attorneys' outraged cries that the provision was intended to
apply to terrorism only, the government pointed to the fact that the
Patriot Act is not, by its terms, limited to terrorism, and appropriate provisions can be applied to any crime. Congress clearly did not
protect Americans from such overreaching when it passed the
Patriot Act. Americans are just waking up to this bait-and-switch
tactic.

ABSENT-MINDED SCIENTIST—OR TERRORIST?

It was an arrest that rocked the American scientific research
community, much as the arrest of Attorney Lynne Stewart troubled attorneys (see chapter 3). In January 2003 federal authorities arrested sixty-two-year-old Thomas Butler, a well-known
researcher of the bubonic plague, on a sixty-nine-count indictment
that included charges that he smuggled plague bacteria and lied to
the Federal Bureau of Investigation (FBI). The government implication was that Butler is a "bioterrorist."

People who know him say the proposition is absurd. Butler's case
stems from a report he made in January that thirty vials of plague
bacteria had gone missing from his lab at Texas Tech University. He
said he presumed them stolen. The FBI and the Lubbock Police
Department sent sixty investigators to scour the university and
town in search of the missing vials. Under intense interrogation,
Butler signed a statement that he had actually destroyed the vials
and had lied to the FBI about their disappearance. Since then, Butler has said that he signed only under duress—pressured by the FBI

to reassure the public that there was no danger—after twenty-four hours of intense questioning. He has recanted his confession and pleaded not guilty to all the charges.[9] Supporters say he, like many scientists, is lax about reporting and record keeping, but none think he did anything untoward with the vials of toxic microbes. Colonel W. Russell Byrne,[10] a bacteriologist at the U.S. Army Research Institute of Infectious Diseases at Fort Detrick, Maryland, wrote to the prosecutor in Butler's case, lauding the scientist's character but also noting his sometimes-casual approach to the bureaucratic details of his dangerous work.

A provision of the 1996 Public Health Service Act—the statute Butler is accused of violating—made filling out customs forms and keeping precise records a strict requirement. The USA Patriot Act added criminal sanctions for violations of record keeping and security requirements set out in hundreds of pages of regulations. A jury acquitted Butler of terrorism charges but found him guilty of falsifying some lab documents and lying to his university. He will never conduct research again, and perhaps that is fair and just. But a "terrorist" he is not. Yet that is how he will be remembered. (See afterword for update.)

At least two other scientists have also been pursued by Ashcroft. In 2003 Tomas Foral, a graduate student at the University of Connecticut, was charged under the Patriot Act with illegal possession of anthrax held in cold storage. Foral admitted to unknowingly violating the law and, in a plea bargain, was ordered to perform community service. Steven Hatfill, a former military biodefense researcher, was named a "person of interest" by the Justice Department in the 2001 anthrax mailings. Hatfill has denied all wrongdoing and has not been charged. Scientists see the crackdown on Hatfill as just the beginning of the government stymieing science in the name of fighting terror. Recently, Chinese scientists were denied visas to attend an academic conference in the United States. The government claimed they did not get their paperwork done in a timely manner; speculation is that the conference content (defending against bioterrorism) was deemed too "sensitive" to allow Chinese participation. The National Academy of Sciences has condemned the scrutiny of scientists as impeding scientific progress. Certainly, it also is counterproductive to the government's self-proclaimed efforts to have the world join in its war on terror. (See afterword for updates.)

New Crimes, New Surveillance Laws

In addition to making garden-variety crimes (albeit serious ones) crimes of terror, the government is using the powers of the USA Patriot Act to conduct surveillance in a way not possible in a pre–September 11 world. With "sneak-and-peek" warrants, roving wiretaps, and access to records from medical institutions, businesses, Internet service providers, and libraries, the government has been able to prosecute crimes previously impossible to prosecute without breaking down the walls of the Fourth Amendment. A study in January 2003 by the General Accounting Office, the investigative arm of Congress, concluded that while the number of terrorism investigations at the Justice Department soared after the September 11 attacks, 75 percent of the convictions that the department classified as "international terrorism" were wrongly labeled.[11] Many dealt with more common crimes such as document forgery. Senator Patrick Leahy (D-VT) shared the sentiments of a few lawmakers and civil libertarians who felt they had been hoodwinked into giving up the Bill of Rights in the name of fighting terrorism.[12]

YOUR BANK AND YOU

Regulations under the USA Patriot and Homeland Security acts reached stockbrokers in 2002 and local banking institutions in 2003.

The Patriot Act requires brokers and dealers in securities to train their personnel in procedures to track "suspicious" customers. The requirements are not limited to "terrorist" financing or money laundering but apply generically to "suspicious" activity. The government can easily obtain financial records from banking institutions if it avers that a customer is engaging in "suspicious" activity that may harm the government. Section 314 of the Patriot Act is broadly written to cover not just terrorist financing but any criminal wrongdoing. A National Association of Securities Dealers 2002 compliance manual tells its employees to report "suspicious" people and transactions to the government. "Red flags" of suspicion should be raised, for instance, when "customers are overly concerned with reporting requirements and are reluctant to provide requested information"; when the transaction makes no "business sense" to the broker; and when the customer has a "questionable background" or is the subject of news reports suggesting possible criminal activity. The broker or employee who fails to file a "suspicious activity report" with the appropriate authorities is liable for prosecution.[13]

Regulations applicable to banks and savings and loan institutions went into effect in October 2003. Banks must check the government's many watch lists and must not open accounts or accept deposits from persons on the lists. In some cases, the person's presence must be reported immediately to the federal authorities. In a further reach, all professionals involved in real estate closings, including mortgage companies, attorneys, and title companies, must not conduct a closing with anyone on a government list. To do so subjects the professional to criminal sanctions. The lists contain tens of thousands of names. There is no way a person can ascertain if he or she is on the list. And if a person's name is on the list erroneously (say, because the person has the same name as a suspicious person), there is no mechanism for getting removed from the list. The chances of being denied the privilege of opening a bank account or buying a home are great. Worse, the meaning of "suspicious"

activity that might get someone reported to the authorities is subjective, and can and will lead to people being wrongfully denied their
right to conduct business and deal with their assets.

THE FBI IS WATCHING THE WEB

Cryptome is a Web site dedicated to investigating and publishing
accounts of government improprieties, particularly as they relate
to secrecy and First Amendment violations. On November 4, 2003,
FBI agents visited the Web site's New York office and met with site
owner John Young. The agents said that they had information that
the Web site was a source of information that could be used to
"harm the United States." Prior investigations by the FBI, the agent
admitted, had not found any evidence of criminal wrongdoing, but
the FBI was fearful that information on the site would end up in
the "wrong" hands. Cryptome was asked to report to the FBI any
"gut feeling" that the information posted could be a "threat" to the
United States.[14]

One agent said that visits such as these are increasingly common as the government seeks out information on threats to the
United States. The agents said they would "write up" a report on
their visit—what they would write would not be disclosed, of
course. The agents asked Young that their names not be published,
but Cryptome refused to honor that request. One reason for their
anonymity request is so that information about them could not be
pulled from one of many databases available online. Government
agents do not want data mining used on them, obviously. Cryptome
has a host of documents on its Web site, most of which are government documents obtained from various sources. The site says it
will not remove any document without a valid court order, and no
order has ever been served on them.

In October 2003 foreign Web sites appeared on the State Department's list of "terrorist organizations." Visits to Web sites are easy

for the government to monitor with "spyware"—computer pro-grams that disclose the Internet addresses of people accessing a Web site. And Web site owners can, to some degree, monitor the gov-ernment's watching of them. Owners of sites that print anti-admin-istration views have reported that they are routinely tracked by visitors with government military or intelligence e-mail addresses.

LOSS OF ACADEMIC FREEDOM

In October 2003 proposed legislation passed the House of Repre-sentatives that that allows federal oversight of university and col-lege academic departments that involve international topics and students. An amendment to Title VI of the U.S. Code creates an International Education Advisory Board that will consult with agencies in the Department of Homeland Security to help ensure that academics are not "undermining" American foreign policy.[15] At the time this book went to press, the bill still had to pass the Senate, but passage seemed likely. Academics warn that this signals the end of academic freedom and the beginning of government meddling in higher education, long a province of totalitarian regimes such as China.

TOTAL INFORMATION AWARENESS

Admiral John Poindexter, who under President Ronald Reagan was involved in the Iran-Contra scandal, was hired by the Pentagon to develop an infrastructure for compiling databases on American cit-izens. Named Total Information Awareness (TIA), Poindexter said that the system would be capable of aggregating all available elec-tronic information on citizens, including medical and financial records, to create individual profiles. The government could then target individuals who might be engaged in something the govern-ment wanted to thwart based on the profile report, ostensibly in the name of fighting terror. Think of the database as providing an "in-search-of" advertisement: in search of petite redhead who has a sharp tongue and writes about John Ashcroft; likes dogs and gardening; listens to everything from Brahms to blues; may not be armed, but should be considered dangerous. Search the database for all redheads with one or two of the "points" on the profile, then sweep in on the suspects. Detain for questioning. Find something they have done wrong in the past, charge them with the maximum offense, threaten with enemy combatant status if they don't plead guilty, sentence redheads to ten years in prison. Think this is far-fetched? How did the government round up foreign immigrants with visas? Immigration authorities simply check criminal records databases, pull up records, and take actions against permanent resident aliens who fit certain profiles.

When the word got out that TIA funding was an item in the defense budget, a few members of Congress reacted negatively. They pulled the plug on the project and strongly suggested that Poindexter be sent packing. In the summer of 2003, Poindexter left the Pentagon. But TIA was not gone. It reappeared under another name, MATRIX (Multistate Anti-Terrorism Information Exchange). Matrix is an interstate electronic database started by the state of Florida. Florida set out to get other states involved by pooling their criminal databases. Other databases would be added to law enforcement records. In October 2003 the American Civil Liberties Union (ACLU) filed simultaneous Freedom of Information Act (FOIA) requests in Connecticut, Michigan, New York, Ohio, and Pennsylvania about those states' participation in the new Matrix database surveillance system. "Congress killed the Pentagon's 'Total Information Awareness' data mining program, but now the federal government is trying to build up a state-run equivalent," said Barry Steinhardt, director of the ACLU's Technology and Liberty Program. "In essence, the government is replacing an unpopular Big Brother initiative with a lot of little brothers," he added, noting that the program is receiving twelve million dollars from the departments of Justice and Homeland Security. "What does it take for the message to get through that government spying on the activities of innocent Americans will not be tolerated?"[16] The ACLU's requests, which were filed under individual states' open-records laws, come on the heels of a federal FOIA request it filed October 17, 2003. A similar request was also filed in Florida, where the program originated. The goal of the requests is to find out what information sources the system is drawing upon—which information program officials have refused to disclose—as well as who has access to the database and how it is being used.

According to congressional testimony and news reports, Matrix creates dossiers about individuals from government databases and private-sector information companies that compile files on Americans' activities for profit. It then makes those dossiers available for search by federal and state law enforcement officers. In addition, Matrix workers comb through millions of files in search of "anomalies" that may be indicative of terrorist or other criminal activity. While company officials have refused to disclose details of the program, according to news reports, the kind of information that can be searched includes credit histories, driver's license photographs, marriage and divorce records, Social Security numbers, dates of birth, and the names and addresses of family members, neighbors, and business associates.

Raising even more issues for critics, the Matrix is operated by a private company, Seisint Inc. of Boca Raton, Florida. Ironically, the company's founder was forced to resign after information about his own past came to light: according to Florida police, he was formerly a drug smuggler and piloted multiple planes carrying cocaine from Colombia to the United States.

As a result of ACLU publicity, six states went on record as declining to join the project. The state of Georgia withdrew from the program after public outcry. But in January 2004 it was disclosed that

Georgia law enforcement agents had been secretly feeding data into the Matrix database. Governor Sonny Perdue promised that Georgia's participation would cease.[17] Participating states as of publication of this book are Florida, Pennsylvania, Connecticut, Michigan, New York, and Ohio.

The America We Have Become

> Every day, law enforcement personnel and intelligence officers are tracking terrorist threats; analysts are examining airline passenger lists; the men and women of our new Homeland Security Department are patrolling our coasts and borders. And their vigilance is protecting America.

> —PRESIDENT BUSH, State of the Union Address, January 20, 2004[18]

The way the president sees it, his administration's strategies in the war on terror are protecting the American people. Civil libertarians look at these tactics through a different lens. In a report aptly titled "Insatiable Appetite," the ACLU summarized the challenges to the American way of life occasioned by the government's response to the events of September 11 as threats to dissent, liberty, equality, constitutional checks and balances, open government, and the rule of law.[19]

Examples of these threats are legion—and we have discussed many of them in the preceding chapters. The administration has squelched dissent among citizens and countries by stating without equivocation that "you" are either "for us" or "against us." And, if you are "against us," you are a terrorist. This argument was used against countries who did not join the "coalition of the willing" to depose Saddam Hussein. It was repeated by administration officials and commentators when Bush went before Congress in October

2003 to ask for eighty-seven billion dollars to continue to fight the war in Iraq (which was supposed to have ended months before). Congress gave him almost all that he asked for; but the few who questioned line items in the proposed budget were often shouted down by the conservative media cabal, such as Ann Coulter, as supporting terrorism.[20] There was no room, it appeared, for debate, let alone dissent, in a post–September 11 world. But without dissent, liberty is a hollow promise. Without dissent a government's wrongs can never be debated and righted.

In terms of equality, people from Arab and Muslim backgrounds are the new victims of guilt by association. As lawyers such as Ashraf Nubani and David Cole have pointed out, if you are a Muslim or Arab today in America, there is no justice. In a personal communication to me, Nubani told of a federal judge who commented in the course of a trial of one of his Muslim clients that "all terrorists are liars."[21] Perhaps what the judge meant to say was that all Arabs and Muslims are "liars." In either case, it's a prejudicial comment and one unbecoming a federal judge.

Before September 11, Islam was the one of the world's fastest-growing religions. In the United States and in the rest of the world, Islamic schools and mosques were proliferating, and Muslims were playing an increasingly important role in the highest levels of academia and government. Given the treatment of Muslims and Arabs in the massive questionings and detentions after September 11, one wonders if the United States can ever again have a good relationship with Muslims at home or abroad. As Cole told me, the government, by its very policies, has alienated the very people it should have been strengthening ties with—Arabs and Muslims, active members of American society, who love America.[22] It has done this primarily through prosecuting minor offenses and deporting scores of Muslims because of their association with Muslim or Arab causes. The detention of thousands of immigrants on the pretext of investigating ties to terrorism has opened a huge chasm between the Muslim community and the Bush administration. Ironically, many Muslims supported Bush in the 2000 presidential election, a decision almost universally regretted now in that community.[23] It has also been suggested that the tough immigration policies set in place after September 11 will lock out much of the brainpower from foreign countries that contributed greatly to the technology boom of the 1990s.[24] Making it hard to get into the country in the name of keeping out terrorists seems like a high price to pay for a society that thrives on openness and unlimited opportunity, just as sacrificing liberty in the name of security seems like a bad bargain.

Apparently not content to humiliate the Muslim and Arab communities in Lackawanna, New York, with the prosecution of six men for being a "terrorist cell" (some pleaded to having briefly visited an al Qaeda training camp; see chapter 2) in October 2003, two hundred law enforcement officers representing fifty law enforcement agencies arrested twenty Arab men in the Lackawanna and Buffalo communities on drug charges. Mohamed Albanna, vice president of the American Muslim Council of Western New York, wondered if the number of police officials used in this operation indicated that the Arab American community was getting "extra scrutiny." In an editorial playing down the ramifications of selective prosecution, the *Buffalo News* reminded its readers to not forget the prosecution of the Lackawanna "cell." [25] What does that have to do with drug arrests? Indeed, Arabs and Muslims, as we have seen throughout the book, have been charged with minor violations of the law years after the offenses. The reason the government so often charged Muslims with lying on visa applications (and the lies included saying you were "single" instead of "divorced" or saying you had not been convicted of a crime, when you had, but it had been overturned on appeal) was because any fraud conviction, no matter how minor, makes even a legal resident instantly deportable. The same deportation possibilities apply in the drug-related crimes for which the Buffalo-area men were arrested. Blacks have experienced this kind of prejudice for two hundred years—guilt by skin color, by neighborhood. The new "whipping boys" are now Arabs and Muslims.

ARE THESE UNPRECEDENTED TIMES?

New York attorney Stanley Cohen has devoted a lifetime in the legal profession to fighting unpopular causes. He has represented dozens of defendants charged with terrorism, and openly criticizes John Ashcroft and his prosecutors. Taking the long view of the current status of the law, Cohen challenges the notion that times such as these are "unprecedented." He refers to the Palmer raids, McCarthyism, and the internment of the Japanese during World War II as evidence that the targeting of people by ethnicity and affiliation and the stifling of political dissent is nothing new. In a speech given at Portland State University in August 2003, Cohen noted that for ten years, Muslims have been under fire because of the Zionist lobby. For ten years, he said, there has been secret surveillance, attacks on Muslim communities, and attacks on the Islamic charities, many of which were finally put out of business by the government post–September 11. For most of the ten years, the attacks were covert; now they are overt, says Cohen.[26]

Others share Cohen's view that these are not exactly unprecedented times. Cole likens the current war on terror to the cold war, in which the enemies were nations, to be sure, but they were enemies precisely because the United States feared their ideology and culture. The raids of which Cohen speaks were undertaken in the name of that war, and many of the clients that Cole represented in the 1970s were ideological enemies of the U.S. government because they favored unpopular political causes that were all lumped under the umbrella of "communism."[27]

What few have mentioned is the unprecedented way in which President Bush has taken the power of the executive branch of government to new heights (or depths depending on one's perspective). Most Oval Office watchers say that Bush came into his own during the aftermath of the September 11 attacks. He certainly did. Author Gore Vidal pointed out that the structure of our government actually enabled Bush to attempt to lead the United States into an eternal war in the name of national security.[28] Invoking executive-branch war powers gives the president a legal cover for the suspension of civil liberties, such as Abraham Lincoln's suspension of the writ of habeas corpus during the Civil War. The Bush administration also has a penchant for secrecy, and it has used it frequently in its "war" effort. Secret arrests and trials utilizing secret evidence, secret terrorist watch lists, and secret federal court dockets ensure one certain result—unaccountability. And unaccountability is the stuff of despots, not democracies.

ARE WE FOREVER CHANGED?

Few could have anticipated that the war on terror, announced in the aftermath of the tragedy of September 11, would become a war on American citizens and resident aliens, a war on freedom, and a war on the Constitution itself. Given terrorism will never be entirely stamped out, we have grave reason to fear that the war will last until the end of time and that life as we knew it prior to September 11 will never exist again.

When Congress allowed the USA Patriot Act to pass virtually without debate and most members did not even read a law that made such sweeping changes in freedom, the concept of congressional oversight of the executive branch ended. When federal judge after federal judge handed the administration victory after victory and authorized detentions without charge, charges without trials, trials without attorneys, and trials with secret evidence, the concept of the judicial oversight of the executive branch ended. For all intents and purposes, our constitutional systems of three independent branches of government has ended. There is only one branch of government—an all-powerful president.

Even if the war on terror was to be won tomorrow, the freedoms that Americans have given up, or those that have been wrested from them by a complicit Congress and judiciary, are not likely to be regained. Why? Because whatever party is in control, whoever leads this country will have much to gain from retaining the powers grabbed by the Bush administration. What government would not like to conduct its business in total secrecy? What judge would not like to exclude the press and public from its deliberations?

A Lot of Questions, Few Answers

More than two years after the tragic day that changed America as we know it, there are few answers to questions about who was involved in the attacks, who in the U.S. government knew or had reason to know about them in advance, and what exactly was known. Congress created a special panel to investigate September 11, whose members were approved by President Bush, but the White House was slow to cooperate. (See afterword for updates.) Frustrated, late in 2003, a family member of a victim of the attack filed a suit against President Bush alleging that he had done nothing to protect the country against attacks, after he had been given warnings that they were possible.[29] Also named were Secretary of Defense Donald Rumsfeld, Attorney General Ashcroft, and others.

Along with unanswered questions come vague predictions of new attacks from our government. Already Bush has made the war on terror a central focus of his reelection campaign. As we noted above, in his January 2004 State of the Union address, he reminded the country that "we are at war." In an interview with Tim Russert on *Meet the Press* on February 8, 2004, Bush said, "I am a wartime president."[30] Presenting himself as a wartime leader challenges

Americans to not change generals in midbattle. A Bush reelection-campaign television advertisement depicts Ground Zero on September 11 and urges viewers to vote for "steady leadership in times of change." [31]

Without answers to hard questions and without government accountability for the part it might have played in not preventing the attacks (notably by failing to carry out the laws that were in place to protect against terrorist activities), Americans are as vulnerable to attack as they were before September 11, perhaps more so because of the unfair treatment of foreign citizens and the mistreatment of those on U.S. soil. Foreign policy experts, such as retired General Brent Scowcroft, who served as national security advisor to former presidents Ronald Reagan and George H. W. Bush, had warned against the United States invading Iraq, beginning a war that Bush now claims is part of the war on terror. Scowcroft argued that the war will make the Middle East more dangerous and will undermine the global war on terrorism by diverting funds and forces. [32] His warning, and those of other experienced foreign relations and national security experts, has been proven prescient. Bitterness created by the war in Iraq has opened the door for rival factions, perhaps even al Qaeda, to target American soldiers and Iraqi citizens working with Coalition forces.

No amount of code orange alerts, of sky marshals on airplanes, and of increased security in public buildings is going to make us safe when we don't know the truth of how and why September 11 happened in the first place. The September 11 commission may be successful in "connecting the dots," in spite of constant resistance and obstructions from the Bush administration. As this book went to press, the spring 2004 deadline for the panel's completion of its work had been extended, but only by two months. And that extension was a huge concession from the Republicans, who balked at any extension at all. Even with an extension, the panel's hands were tied by the Bush administration's recalcitrance. Condaleeza Rice appeared before the panel, bowing to public pressure. President Bush agreed to answer questions only with Vice President Cheney by his side. Clearly, the Bush administration was far from giving the panel its promised "full cooperation." What are we to make of this? Does the administration have something to hide about what it knew about the September 11 attacks and when it knew it? Or was it just being true to its passion for secrecy at all costs?

Of the more long-lasting implications is this hard truth: the Bush administration's war on civil liberties (under the guise of a war on terror) is a war against the law and the rule of law. The framers of the Constitution and the proponents of the Bill of Rights feared as much when they deliberately debated, drafted, and fine-tuned the constitutional compact between the governed and the government, which has thus far stood the test of time. What an irony if one administration can use a tragedy like September 11 to turn back the clock and establish the type of rule—despotism— that our founding fathers risked their lives and fortunes to escape.

In an interview with Larry King on December 18, 2002, Attorney General Ashcroft said, "We're in the business of securing freedom, not sacrificing freedom."[33] The words have an eerie ring to them. Freedom is not a business. And freedom is not Ashcroft's to either "secure" or "sacrifice." Rather, to use President Bush's words, "Freedom is God's gift to the world." Let's take the president at his word and claim the promise of freedom—not as guaranteed by George Bush, John Ashcroft, or, with all due respect, even God, but as promised to us by the Bill of Rights. It has weathered 213 years of political vicissitudes and a civil war. It can withstand the assault of Ashcroft and Bush as long as each and every American settles for nothing less than leaders and laws that support, not undermine, freedom's very existence.

AFTERWORD

Chronicling a moving target like the Bush administration's war on civil liberties is a frustrating and depressing task. Frustrating because the war may, by its very terms, never end, and depressing because the Constitution and the American people are losing more battles than they are winning.

At the time this book went to press, many of the issues examined in the preceding chapters were being played out in the courts, while new matters not examined in this book were being revealed. The following are some significant events that took place between February and April 2004, including both updates to cases and issues previously discussed in the book and new assaults on our civil liberties:

❖ In April 2004, President Bush began to make the Patriot Act a central focus of his reelection campaign. During the week of April 19, he made speeches in Pennsylvania and New York in which he touted the importance of the law in fighting terrorism.

He called for the renewal of all provisions that were set to expire
in 2005 (see chapter 1). Said President Bush, "The Patriot Act
defends our liberty. The Patriot Act makes it able for those of
us in positions of responsibility to defend the liberty of the
American people. It's essential law." Democratic presidential
candidate Senator John Kerry accused Bush of misleading the
public into thinking that the Patriot Act could make up for the
intelligence failures that led to the September 11 attacks. Kerry
said that the administration has "used the Patriot Act in ways
that were never intended and for reasons that have nothing to
do with terrorism" (see chapter 7). Bush criticized Kerry's position on the Patriot Act in campaign ads, accusing Kerry of "waf-
fling" on the law that he voted for. Kerry responded that he was
for much of the law, but wanted the provisions aimed at spying
on ordinary Americans repealed.[1] On April 22, 2004, the ACLU
challenged President Bush's "misinformation" about the Patriot
Act in a point-by-point rebuttal posted on its Web site.[2]

❖ On April 21, a bill was introduced in the House of Representatives (HR 2934, the "Terrorist Penalties Enhancement Act of
2003") that would expand the definitions of terrorism so that
some twenty-three existing federal crimes could qualify for the
death penalty. Further, crimes that provide for more than one
year in prison upon conviction could become capital offenses if
they fall within a proposed expanded definition of domestic terrorism and cause someone's death. As discussed in chapters 1
and 7, the definitions of terrorism are so broad that lawful
protest that inadvertently, even remotely, is involved with the
death of someone (e.g., a political protest that impedes an ambulance, if the patient dies as a result of delay in treatment), could
mean the death penalty for the protestor.[3]

❖ The Bush administration began to release some prisoners from
Guantanamo Bay, Cuba, with the understanding that the pris-

oners' home countries would prosecute them for terrorism. On March 9, 2004, when the United States released five British citizens from Guantanamo Bay, the government of Great Britain, our staunchest ally in the war in Iraq, took the men into custody, as was their agreement with the U.S. government, then promptly released them, saying that they had no cause to hold them as they had not committed any crime under Britain's anti-terrorism laws. Naturally, this called into question why they were detained by the United States in the first place.[4] Meanwhile, some of the prisoners released to Spain and Russia feared that they would be tortured and executed when returned home.[5] If Bush and Rumsfeld thought they could have convicted these prisoners, you can bet they would have kept and tried them. The logical conclusion is that the men and boys released are not the terrorists the administration thought they were. Yet their lives are likely ruined, given the stigma (not to mention the trauma) of being held prisoner for more than two years and being identified by the United States as "terrorists" who might have had something to do with the September 11 attacks.

Speaking of lives being affected, an Afghan boy, Ismail Agha, now fifteen, who was captured by U.S. forces when he was thirteen, spent two years in Guantanamo and was released January 29, 2004. It was reported that he was happy that he had learned to speak English and to read, but was relieved to be home with his family. In a story corroborated by his father, the boy said that he had left the family home the day of his capture to find work, only to be picked up and sent to Guantanamo. He said that his keepers at Guantanamo warned him upon his release that if he ever got "arrested" again, he would go to prison for life. Arrested again? The United States had no cause to arrest him the first time, and doubtless the American military believed him to be harmless or he would not have been released. For, according to a Pentagon spokesman, the boy was not released because of his age, which, the source is quoted as saying, "matters not" when it comes to enemy combatants.[6] Upon his release, Agha learned that his family had never received the letters he sent them from prison.

The Pentagon also announced that it was continuing to prepare for trials of several Guantanamo detainees by military tribunals, though it refused to say when the trials would take place and what the charges would be. It was "loosening" some of its own rules of engagement against the military attorneys who would be defending the men, including no longer allowing prosecutors to listen in on attorney-client conversations, but rather appointing security officers to do so. The Pentagon also announced that many of the current detainees, and those who might be brought to Guantanamo in the future, may be incarcerated there for years, even indefinitely, as long as the government felt it was necessary to protect Americans at home and its troops at war.[7] This would include prisoners who were tried and served out their sentences as well as those never brought to trial, and it could extend beyond the declared "end" of the war on terror (whenever that might be).[8] The Pentagon also announced, in a display of generosity, that the government was rewriting the "rules" (that President George W. Bush and Attorney General John Ashcroft had crafted) to allow detainees held at Guantanamo the opportunity, once a year, to question their further detention.[9] The board would be named by Secretary of Defense Donald Rumsfeld and approved by Congress. The Pentagon made it clear, however, that the prisoners' rights to a hearing would be solely at its discretion and that it could disband the panel and the hearings at any time. The Pentagon announcement referred to the reviewing body as a "parole board" of sorts—an odd moniker given that parole is a procedure that comes when a prisoner has served a portion of a prison term and is released early. Military law experts say that the entire scheme surrounding the Guantanamo Bay prisoners—their capture,

detention, plans (or not) for trials, and indefinite imprisonment—is unprecedented, except among countries whose human
and civil rights abuses are denounced by the civilized world.

For the prisoners who will never be charged, let alone tried,
being treated as if they were convicts pretty much sums up the
administration's stance toward them—guilt without charge,
incarceration without sentence. Parole boards are generally
stacked with political appointees who do the bidding of the governor or attorney general. Rumsfeld's "parole" boards are likely
to be even more of a sham than their correctional counterparts.

On April 20, 2004, the Supreme Court heard oral arguments
in the cases of the Guantanamo Bay prisoners. Though it is
impossible to divine the justices' thinking, the tone of the questioning seemed to suggest that at least five would support federal court habeas corpus review of the enemy combatants'
detention.

❖ The government continues to win some and lose some in terms
of the trials of alleged terrorists. Among the cases discussed in
chapter 2 was that of the Alexandria Eleven. Four of the men
gave up a jury trial, assuming they could not get a fair jury in
the Alexandria, Virginia, federal court. Because they would not
plead guilty, the Neutrality Act charges against them were
replaced with terrorism charges under the Patriot Act. Though
they thought they were fortunate to draw Judge Leonie
Brinkema (see chapter 2) as presiding judge, only one of the four
fared well. On March 4, 2004, Judge Brinkema found three of
the men guilty of conspiring to wage war against the United
States abroad.[10] Early in the trial, Brinkema had dismissed the
charges against one of the men. In dismissing that case, she
noted that the government's allegation that playing paintball
signified preparing to engage in terrorism was not, in and of
itself, enough to proceed against him. Thousands of children

and adults play paintball, she reasoned. Yet, playing paintball did play into her decision to find the other three guilty (each of whom faces fifty to one hundred years in prison). One of the three men had been offered a plea bargain that would have had him serve two years in prison. Here is what attorney Ashraf Nubian, who was involved in the case, said about the verdict:

> This trial was a trial of Islam as a religion. After September 11 Attorney General Ashcroft compared his mission in fighting terrorism to Robert Kennedy's mission in fighting the Mafia. The then Attorney General was going after those who "spat on the sidewalk." Ashcroft can take pride in the fact that he has terrorized these Muslims and their families for less than that. Irrespective of Judge Brinkema's verdict, the Government engaged in targeting, coercion, embellishing on half truths, and selective prosecution. America is not safer because three family men who have not committed a single crime face minimum sentences of 50 years plus. Their actions were not criminal and had they been Irish Americans or Israeli Americans engaging in the same paintball activity no one would have been tried, much less convicted. Those who pled guilty found themselves in a situation where pleading guilty spared them their entire lives in prison. Some sold their conscience. Others did not.[11]

✛ On April 22, 2004, the 4th Circuit Court of Appeals rejected Judge Brinkema's sanctions against the government for not allowing Zacarias Moussaoui's attorneys to question government witnesses it is holding in undisclosed locations (see chapter 2). A 2-1 decision of the panel instructed Brinkema to prepare written statements of witness testimony—prepared by the government—and have them read to the jury. Depositions of the witnesses would not be allowed, so Moussaoui would have not right of cross-examination. Further, Brinkema was ordered to instruct the jury that the statements of the witnesses—again, prepared by the government—were reliable. Clearly this decision is a frontal attack on Moussaoui's Sixth Amendment rights. As of this writing Moussaoui's attorneys had not indicated whether they would appeal the ruling to the Supreme Court, or ask for a rehearing of their case in front of a full panel of justices. They appeared to be less troubled by the decision than this author, as the opinion did suggest that the attorneys could take the depositions of government witnesses who were abroad and not in federal custody. Attorney General John Ashcroft rightly boasted that it was a big win for the government.[12]

❖ The government dropped the charges against James Ujaama (see chapter 2) that accused him of setting up and running a Taliban training camp in Oregon. Instead, based on his admission that he provided computers and, through a Web site he was involved with, a recruit to the Taliban in Afghanistan, a federal judge accepted his plea of aiding terrorists and sentenced him to two years in prison in exchange for his agreement to cooperate with prosecutors.[13]

The remaining defendants in the Portland Seven cases were sentenced (see chapter 2). Maher Hawash, Ahmed Bilal, and Muhammad Bilal, who all tried unsuccessfully to join the Taliban, were sentenced to seven, ten, and eight years, respectively, for conspiracy to wage war on the United States.[14]

❖ The Detroit cell case (see chapter 2) took another strange twist. As we have seen, in December 2003 U.S. District Court Judge Gerald Rosen was deciding whether to throw out the jury verdicts and order a new trial after it was disclosed that the prosecutors had, indeed, withheld evidence from the defendants, evidence that could have helped them discredit the government's star witness (whom Attorney General Ashcroft publicly praised, even when doing so—twice—amounted to flagrant violations of Judge Rosen's gag order on both sides). The chief prosecutor in the case, Assistant U.S. Attorney Richard Convertino of Detroit, accused the Justice Department of "gross mismanagement" of the war on terrorism in a lawsuit filed February 13, 2004, in federal court in Washington. Convertino is seeking damages under the Privacy Act, alleging he was subjected to an internal investigation as retaliation for his cooperation with a Senate committee investigating the department's handling of terrorism cases, and that information from the internal probe was wrongly leaked to news media.[15]

✴ The Justice Department's investigation of Convertino parallels the treatment of attorney Jesselyn Radack (see chapter 3). Recall that she was investigated when she disclosed that the government had not provided all of the e-mails it had received from her over the course of its interrogation of John Walker Lindh. At the time this book went to press, Radack herself was considering suing the Justice Department and Ashcroft for retaliating against her after she alerted the prosecutor and the media that her bosses had not obeyed a federal court order.[16] This Justice Department wants its dirty little secrets kept from federal judges and Congress—and it seems to have no end of dirty tricks as payback for employees who don't go along with its subversion of the law.

Not content to make her unemployable as an attorney since it besmirched her reputation, the government has placed Radack on its Transportation Security Administration (TSA) "selectee," list, that catalog of tens of thousands of Americans who find themselves undergoing extra scrutiny when they try to board an airplane. The ACLU suspects that a place on the list is reserved for government dissidents (its executive director is on the list). Radack was challenged recently because she (mother of three, including an infant) was carrying a breast pump ("What's that for?" security agents wanted to know). Her checked baggage was ransacked, but government agents at least left a card telling her that TSA had examined her bag.[17]

✣ The only person convicted of being involved in the September 11 hijackings had his conviction thrown out by a German appeals court. A new trial was ordered in the case of Mounir Motassadeq, a Moroccan citizen.[18] His defense attorneys successfully argued that the U.S. government's refusal to provide access to alleged September 11 mastermind Ramzi Binalshibh, who is in secret U.S. custody, denied their client access to exculpatory evidence. A German intelligence official testified in the trial of Abdelghani Mzoudi, an alleged accomplice of Motassadeq, that he had seen reports that Binalshibh denied Motassadeq's involvement in the tragedy. Mzoudi was acquitted. The U.S. government's failure to make Binalshibh available to the lawyers for Zacarias Moussaoui, the only person on trial for the September 11 attacks in U.S. courts, led Judge Brinkema to rule that federal prosecutors could not try to tie Moussaoui to September 11 and could not seek the death penalty (see chapter 2 and update above). It is likely that Judge Brinkema had access to the same information the German judges had. It is fair to assume that if Binalshibh had information that would have helped the German or American courts convict these men, the U.S. government would have produced Binalshibh as its own star witness. Prosecutors' refusal to assist the German court left German prosecutors frustrated and vowing not to bring any other charges if U.S. cooperation was needed.

✣ Former Texas Tech University professor Thomas Butler (see chapter 7) was sentenced to two years in prison and fined $15,000. He also had to turn in his medical license and was

forced to retire from the university. The scientist was charged
with, but not convicted of, shipping plague tissue samples out
of the country for use as bioterrorism. He was found guilty of
mislabeling the package and exporting the samples without
approval from the U. S. government.[19]

✣ On April 28, 2004, the Supreme Court heard oral arguments in
the appeals of Jose Padilla and Yaser Hamdi (see chapter 2). On
March 3, 2004, the government allowed Padilla's court-appointed
attorneys, Donna Newman and Andrew Patel, to visit Padilla in
the Navy brig in Charleston, South Carolina. But it was not the
usual attorney-inmate visit. Newman and Padilla were separated
by a glass partition, and government officials watched their every
move, listened to their every word, and videotaped their meeting. Newman wryly noted that she was looking forward to future
government invitations to meet with her client.[20] The government did the same favor for Yaser Hamdi, allowing federal
defender Frank Dunham (also the attorney for Zacarias Moussaoui) to visit his client in a Norfolk navy jail.

✣ By refusing to grant appeals, the U.S. Supreme Court let stand
decisions of lower federal courts that allowed the government
to conduct certain cases in total secrecy, without so much as an
entry in the court's docket. Lawyers for Mohamed Kamel Bellahouel (see chapter 5) asked the justices to consider whether
lower federal courts acted improperly in keeping the government's case against their client so secret that its mere existence
was revealed only by accident. Civil libertarians see the Court's
refusal to take up the matter as sending a message to the administration that secrecy will be tolerated. The Court apparently
does not agree with the oft-stated belief that secrecy is the death
of democracies.

- The Supreme Court also agreed with a federal court in Texas that refused to allow the Holy Land Foundation for Relief and Development (HLF) to see the evidence the government has against it that led to HLF being placed on the terrorist organization list. The Bush administration has shut down dozens of similar charities and frozen their assets (see chapter 4). Some would say this deprivation of an organization's property is a blatant violation of the Fifth Amendment, which forbids the taking of property without due process of law. The lower courts gave no process at all to HLF or other organizations. The Bush administration said, in effect, "We have you on our list, you shall not see the list, you shall not question the list, and you will not get off the list." The Supreme Court, while not necessarily agreeing with the policy, in effect gave it the green light.

- Sami Al-Arian, the former University of South Florida "terrorist" (according to U.S. prosecutors) professor, was once an FBI informant who was "wired" when meeting with aides in the Clinton and Bush White Houses, it was reported on April 6, 2004. His attorneys want to gain access to the tapes of those meetings, but the government has refused.[21]

- The TSA is having trouble convincing international airlines to accept its Computer Assisted Passenger Prescreening System (CAPPS II) program (see chapter 1). Other countries' flag carriers are far more concerned than our own with the fact that innocent people may be (and already have been) targeted as terrorists and have no way to demand removal from the list.[22] These airlines don't want to share their passenger lists with the TSA. The current CAPPS system calls for airlines to report passenger information to it as soon as seats are booked. The information will be combined with all available computerized information about passengers in an effort to profile them according to security risk level.

❖ International Monetary Fund (IMF) economist and Spanish citizen Alex Segura can tell you why you ought to be worried about airline screening. On March 10, 2003, he was returning to Washington, D.C., from an official mission aboard an Air France plane. As the plane landed, passengers were ordered to stay seated so that Homeland Security Administration agents could board the plane. They made a beeline for Segura, took him off the plane, handcuffed him, and questioned him for three hours before releasing him. All the government would say was that his name and birth date "matched those of a 'dangerous individual' listed in federal security databases." In addition to his passport, Segura showed agents his visa (given to employees of international organizations) as well as his United Nations identification.[23] In an e-mail to employees, IMF personnel manager John Alvey deplored the treatment and said that the IMF was exploring all options to avoid incidents like this, including moving the organization out of the United States.[24]

❖ The National Commission on Terrorist Attacks Upon the United States (also known as the 9-11 Commission), issued a staff statement condemning government targeting of immigrants immediately after September 11 (see chapter 5). It concluded that not one of the hundreds of Arab and Muslim men held for weeks, even months, had been shown to have any ties to the attacks on September 11 or terrorism.[25]

❖ In a report that would be hilarious if it were not at once stupid and alarming, the Department of Homeland Security has warned that pressure cookers—the kind that this author has in her kitchen (and which her mother and grandmother had)—

should be seized if found in the course of a terrorism investigation. Pressure cookers, the memo warned, can explode (no surprise there, if you have ever used one) and thus can be considered instrumentalities of terror.[26]

✣ Although most critics have focused on threats to individual civil liberties, there are also fears that the administration could use the Patriot Act to target organizations that oppose its policies, threatening constitutionally protected speech. For instance, the Department of Justice admits that the FBI is conducting surveillance on certain organizations protesting the war in Iraq, on the grounds that they might be training their members in "terrorist" tactics. In February 2004 the Department of Justice began issuing grand jury subpoenas for individuals who attended a November 2003 antiwar rally at Drake University in Des Moines, Iowa, sponsored by the National Lawyers Guild, an organization that has historically fought for civil liberties and human rights. The government also ordered Drake University to turn over academic records of students who attended the rally and any campus security tapes of the meetings. In addition, the financial and membership records of the National Lawyers Guild were demanded. Recipients of the subpoenas filed motions to quash. On February 10, 2004, the day the federal court in Des Moines, Iowa, was scheduled to hear the motions to quash, the government withdrew most of the subpoenas. Prosecutors said they never meant to "chill" legitimate First Amendment activities, but were only looking for the identity of a person who may have attended the antiwar rally and tried to scale the fence of a National Guard building nearby.[27]

Activists are increasingly aware that the FBI and Department of Justice have been conducting surveillance on antiwar protests and organizational meetings since the planned invasion of Iraq. In 2002 the FBI urged local law enforcement officers to help it

monitor the "suspicious" activities of protestors.[28] The Drake
University subpoenas, however, were the first known grand jury
investigations for engaging in protected First Amendment activities. Clearly, the message from the subpoenas was "Watch out.
We are watching you. And we may investigate, even indict, you."

❖ Beginning with the plans to invade Iraq, some cities and counties began to deny permits for demonstrations or, in places such
as New York City, to make permits nearly impossible to obtain.
On February 27, 2004, a federal judge in Miami, Florida, ruling
on a case brought by the National Lawyers Guild and other
activist organizations, ordered that Miami officials must grant
permission for political protests or, if they deny requests, state
the reason for denial and have a hearing for the applicants to
present their case. People who protested without permits were
being arrested and jailed. In March 2004, constituents of U.S.
Senator Zell Miller (R-GA), including a retired Georgia State
University professor, were arrested and charged with trespass-
ing for events that took place back in November 2002, when
they had refused to leave Miller's Atlanta office. Miller had
repeatedly refused to see them, in spite of repeated efforts on
the protestors' part to arrange a meeting. Their arrests—sixteen months after their failed efforts to meet with their representative—combined with the federal investigations at Drake
University send a clear message to Americans about the loss of
their First Amendment rights of assembly and speech: "Don't
cross this Administration or you will be prosecuted." One of the
Georgia arrestees said, "There's something wrong when our
elected officials would rather arrest us than meet with us." [29]

Several reports about increased surveillance also surfaced in
February 2004: Army intelligence agents attended a conference
on Islamic law held at the University of Texas-Austin and
demanded a roster of attendees and videotapes of sessions; and

local police, acting on behalf of the FBI, conducted surveillance on political activist organizations there.[30]

❖ Despite the efforts of the Bush administration to chill (and even criminally charge) its critics, the number of municipalities and local governments who took official positions against the USA Patriot Act (see chapter 6) continues to grow. As of the end of April 2004, the number was 294 and counting, and included the cities of Pittsburgh and Tampa and four states—Alaska, Hawaii, Maine, and Vermont.[31]

❖ The continued expansion of the word *terrorism* to encompass those who disagree with the government rose to new heights (or sank to new lows) when, late in February, Secretary of Education Rod Paige referred to the National Education Association (NEA) as a terrorist organization. The group earned that name for their "obstructionist and scare" tactics, which were threatening to undermine President Bush's controversial No Child Left Behind Act. Though Paige later called the appellation a poor choice of words, he did not back off from his criticism of the NEA for what he called its disregard for children and education. As discussed in chapter 1, the Patriot Act is broad enough to earn any opponent of the government the label of "terrorist," and Ashcroft has often come close to accusing (and sometimes has outright accused) those who oppose the Patriot Act or his despotic tactics as being "traitors" or "soft on terrorists." But here was Paige, a generally mild-mannered cabinet member, defining as "terrorist" the organization that represents the nation's teachers, simply because the organization disagreed with the administration's education policy.

❖ Former Assistant Attorney General Viet Dinh (see chapter 1), the major crafter of the Patriot Act, said in a February 2004 interview that those who fear the Patriot Act are acting out of ignorance. He encouraged them (us) to take our concerns to our elected officials to try to change the law.[32] Brilliant attorney and law professor that he is, he must surely know how futile those efforts would be. With Bush calling for more "Patriot"-like laws and with his opening campaign ads featuring footage from the wreckage of the World Trade Center, the chance of Congress giving back the rights it took away appear to be slim to none.

❖ A report in the *New York Times* on February 29, 2004, disclosed that the Treasury Department, which maintains a list of terrorist organizations (the National Endowment for the Arts is not yet on the official list), had warned editors and publishers that to alter in any way the manuscript of any person who lives in a country on the U.S. "enemies" list (Syria, Iran, North Korea, Cuba, to name a few) could mean being charged with doing business with the enemy.[33] Never mind if it is a poem or scientific article—insert a comma or correct the syntax and you will be considered to be "trading with the enemy." If prosecuted and convicted, each charge could lead to ten years in prison and a $500,000 fine. It is regulations like these, little known even to the targeted population (editors and publishers) and lesser known to the general public, that demonstrate how a person meaning or doing no harm could be charged with and convicted of being a terrorist or a traitor. The devil is in the details, goes the old maxim, and the devil of this administration is indeed in the regulations that sap civil liberties and mock the Bill of Rights.

❖ Finally, as if to prove the oft-repeated point that one man's terrorist is another man's freedom fighter, an immigration judge in California blocked the deportation of an immigrant who had served a prison term for killing two British soldiers in 1988, finding that Sean O'Cealleagh should not be expelled because his crime was "purely political."[34] Can you imagine a judge saying the same about Arabs or Muslims? They would be deported for spitting on the sidewalk (well, almost).

It will be my continuing frustration not to be able to update this manuscript daily, which is what would be necessary to give readers even a passing chance of keeping up with the Bush administration's continued efforts to dismantle the Bill of Rights. I hope that you, my readers, will be prompted by what you have read here to dedicate yourselves to staying informed about the status of this war on freedom. Doing so will require that you venture outside the mainstream media—what should be known is not going to be found on network or cable news or in local newspapers. An example of the degree to which the press is embedded, even "in bed" with the White House, happened on March 2, 2004,[35] when President Bush invited reporters from CBS, NBC, ABC, Fox, and CNN to talk with him for eighty minutes in the Oval Office—on the condition that they not report on their discussions, quote him, or attribute any information to him. I have to think that reporters worthy of the name would refuse to participate in such an obvious attempt to curry favor with them the day before Bush launched his media campaign for the 2004 elections. Think of that when you watch your favorite nightly news program. National daily papers are not much better informational sources—but some provide a modicum of information, if read faithfully.

In the Resources for Keeping Current section you'll find a list of Web sites to keep you up-to-date on major stories. Diligent readers can subscribe (often at no cost) to e-mail alerts about certain topics. I recommend looking out for any story about John Ashcroft, since it will mainly concern losses of freedom and overstatements of government victories in the war on terrorism. Government secrecy, terrorism prosecutions, and FBI and Justice Department surveillance and monitoring ought to be high on every American's watch list. The government has its watch list of suspected terrorists; we ought to have our own watch list of suspected officials and laws that are subverting our country from the inside—by trampling the Constitution and dismantling the Bill of Rights.

RESOURCES for KEEPING CURRENT

THE FOLLOWING WEB SITES are recommended as sources to continue to keep abreast of changes in the war on civil liberties:

WWW.ACLU.ORG

The American Civil Liberties Union (ACLU) is doing what it does best—defending the Constitution by representing individuals and organizations whose rights have been violated by the government. It has been involved in dozens of cases that have arisen out of the events of September 11 and the war on terror.

WWW.AMNESTY.ORG

Amnesty International works to protect human rights the world over. It has been vocal in protests against the imprisonment of Arab and Muslim individuals as enemy combatants at Guantanamo Bay, Cuba.

HTTP://BABELOGUE.CITYPAGES.COM:8080/ECASSEL/

The author keeps watch over how the Bush administration has been dismantling of the Bill of Rights and other battles in the war on civil liberties.

WWW.CCR-NY.ORG/V2/HOME.ASP

The Center for Constitutional Rights (CCR), like the ACLU, is fighting on the front lines in the war against civil liberties. It has been instrumental in initiating cases discussed in this book, including the recent Ninth Circuit Court of Appeals rulings that portions of the Patriot Act are unconstitutional.

WWW.CRYPTOME.ORG

Cryptome welcomes open, secret, and classified documents for publication that are prohibited by governments worldwide—in particular, material on freedom of expression, privacy, cryptology, dual-use technologies, national security, intelligence, and secret governance (but not limited to those areas). Documents are removed from this site only by order served directly by a U.S. court with jurisdiction.

HTTP://HLP.HOME.IGC.ORG/

The Humanitarian Law Project (HLP) promotes legal and humanitarian solutions to human rights abuses throughout the world. It has been successful in federal suits brought to defend the rights of Arab and Muslim immigrants and citizens who have been victims of the Bush administration's post–September 11 policies. HLP often joins the ACLU and CCR in bringing suits and filing amicus briefs in litigation.

WWW.VILLAGEVOICE.COM/HENTOFF/

The *Village Voice*'s Nat Hentoff has been chronicling the Bush administration's assault on civil liberties. His articles pull no punches in exposing the abuses of the executive branch of government in its assault on the Constitution.

Foreign media often report more on the loss of civil liberties in the United States than American media does. Some especially good reporting can be found on these newspaper Web sites:

The Guardian, http://www.guardian.co.uk

The Observer, http://observer.guardian.co.uk/

The Irish Times, http://www.ireland.com/

ENDNOTES

INTRODUCTION

1. http://www.whitehouse.gov/news/releases/2003/02/counter_terrorism/counter_terrorism_strategy.pdf (accessed March 11, 2004).

2. Bureau of International Information Programs, "Ashcroft Says Terrorism Investigation Aims to Save Lives," U.S. Department of State, December 6, 2001, http://usinfo.state.gov/topical/pol/terror/01120610.htm (accessed February 9, 2004).

3. Sam Stanton and Emily Bazar, "Security Collides with Civil Liberties," *Sacramento Bee*, September 21, 2003, http://www.sacbee.com/content/news/projects/liberty/story/7457444p-8400138c.html (accessed February 9, 2004).

4. Weekly Radio Address, http://www.patriotresource.com/wtc/president/010915a.html (accessed March 11, 2004).

5. Ibid.

6. William Kunstler, "Public Ethics and the Bill of Rights" (commencement address, State University of New York at Buffalo, May 13, 1995). The text of his address is available online at Buffalo Report.com: http://buffaloreport.com/articles/030427kunstler.html (accessed February 9, 2004).

CHAPTER 1 TERRORISM, PATRIOTISM, AND HOMELAND SECURITY

1. Address to Joint Session of Congress and the American People, http://www.whitehouse.gov/news/releases/2001/09/20010920-8.html (accessed March 11, 2004).

2. *Zavala v. Ridge*, 04-00253, reported in Alexei Oreskovic, "Feds Must Respect Bail Ruling on Aliens, Judge Says," *The Recorder*, March 8, 2004, http://www.law.com/jsp/

printerfriendly.jsp?c=LawArticle&t=PrinterFriendlyArticle&cid=1078368930356 (accessed March 9, 2004).

3. http://usinfo.state.gov/usa/infousa/laws/majorlaw/s735_enr.htm (accessed March 11, 2004).

4. State Fair Arena, Oklahoma City, Oklahoma, http://nsi.org/Library/Terrorism/policy.html (accessed March 11, 2004).

5. The USA Patriot Act had amended the statute to increase the penalty from ten years to fifteen years to life.

6. Address to Joint Session of Congress and the American People, http://www.whitehouse.gov/news/releases/2001/09/20010920-8.html (accessed March 11, 2004).

7. Robert O'Harrow, Jr., "Six Weeks in Autumn," *Washington Post*, October 22, 2002, http://www.washingtonpost.com/ac2/wp-dyn/A1999-2002Oct22 (accessed August 3, 2003).

8. Uniting and Strengthening America by Providing Appropriate Tools Required to Intersect and Obstruct Terrorism (USA PATRIOT Act) Act of 2001, Public Law 107-56, 107th Congress, 1st session (October 21, 2001). The full text of the act is available online at the Web site for the Electronic Frontier Foundation: http://www.eff.org/Privacy/Surveillance/Terrorism_militias/20011025_hr3162_usa_patriot_bill.html (accessed February 9, 2004).

9. Elaine Cassel, "The Other War," *City Pages*, April 23, 2003, http://www.citypages.com/databank/24/1168/article11196.asp (accessed February 9, 2004).

10. Norman Oder, "Forum Considers Effect of September 11," *Library Journal*, April 15, 2002, http://www.libraryjournal.com/article/CA206399 (accessed March 11, 2004).

11. Rene Sanchez, "Librarians Make Some Noise Over Patriot Act," *Washington Post*, April 10, 2003, http://foi.missouri.edu/terrorandcivillib/librarians.html (accessed March 11, 2004).

12. http://www.techlawjournal.com/alert/2001/10/03.asp (accessed March 17, 2004).

13. O'Harrow, Jr., "Six Weeks in Autumn."

14. Ibid.

15. For the historical review of the act's passage, I am indebted to C. William Michaels, *No Greater Threat: America After September 11 and the Rise of a National Security State.* (New York: Algora Publishing, 2003), 34.

16. Dan Eggen and Jim Vandehei, "Ashcroft, Patriot Act Trouble Both Liberals and Conservatives," *Miami Herald*, August 29, 2003, http://www.miami.com/mld/miamiherald/news/nation/6645497.htm?template=contentModules/printstory.jsp (accessed October 10, 2003).

17. "Ashcroft: Critics of New Terror Measures Undermine Efforts," CNN.com, December 7, 2001, http://www.cnn.com/2001/US/12/06/inv.ashcroft.hearing/ (accessed August 3, 2003).

18. Office of the Inspector General, "The September 11 Detainees: A Review of the Treatment of Aliens Held on Immigration Charges in Connection with the Investigation of the September 11 Attacks," U.S. Department of Justice, June 2003, http://www.usdoj.gov/oig/special/03-06/analysis.htm (accessed February 9, 2004). For the follow-up report

about Department of Justice responses to the abuses, see Office of the Inspector General, "Supplemental Report on September 11 Detainees' Allegations of Abuse at the Metropolitan Detention Center in Brooklyn, New York," U.S. Department of Justice, December 2003, http://www.usdoj.gov/oig/special/0312/index.htm (accessed February 9, 2004).

19. Eric Lichtblau, "Threats and Responses: The Justice Department; Ashcroft Seeks More Power to Pursue Terror Suspects," *New York Times*, June 6, 2003.

20. The full text of the proposed "Patriot II" is available online as a link in Charles Lewis and Adam Mayle, "Justice Dept. Drafts Sweeping Expansion of Anti-Terrorism Act," Center for Public Integrity, February 7, 2003, http://www.publicintegrity.org/dtaweb/report.asp?ReportID=502&L1=10&L2=10&L3=0&L4=0&L=0 (accessed February 8, 2004).

21. William Safire, "You Are a Suspect," *New York Times*, November 14, 2002, http://www.commondreams.org/views02/1114-08.htm (accessed March 13, 2004).

22. Eric Lichtblau, "Counter-Terrorism Proposals Are a Hard Sell," *New York Times*, September 11, 2003, http://www.nytimes.com/2003/09/11/national/11ASSE.html?th=& pagewanted (accessed September 11, 2003).

23. Cassel, "Brother John's Traveling Patriot Show, Still Not Winning Many Converts," *CounterPunch*, August 30, 2003, http://www.counterpunch.org/cassel08302003.html

24. Proposed law is at http://www.libertythink.com/VICTORYAct.pdf (accessed March 13, 2004).

25. Donn Esmond, "Ashcroft's Methods Hurt His Own Cause," *Buffalo News*, September 9, 2003, http://www.buffalonews.com/editorial/20030909/1005941.asp (accessed September 3, 2003).

26. James Dempsey, Lecture, "The Patriot Act and Other Assaults on Civil Liberties," The American Constitution Society for Law and Policy, Washington, D.C., (October 15, 2003).

27. Dempsey, "The Patriot Act and Other Assaults on Civil Liberties."

28. Viet Dinh and David Cole, interview by Bryant Gumbel, *Flashpoints U.S.A.*, PBS, July 15, 2003. The text of the interview is available online at the PBS Web site: http://www.pbs.org/flashpointsusa/20030715/infocus/topic_03/trans_pat_act.html (accessed August 3, 2003).

29. Dinh and Cole, interview by Bryant Gumbel.

30. Will Lester, "Poll: Terrorism Laws Could Erode Freedoms," *Washington Post*, Outlook Section, September 10, 2003.

31. Jennifer Loven, "Bush Urges More Police Powers Against Terrorists," *Washington Post*, September 10, 2003, http://www.washingtonpost.com/wp-dyn/articles/A55666-2003Sep10.html (accessed September 10, 2003).

32. Homeland Security Act of 2002, Public Law 107-296, 107th Congress, 2nd session. (November 25, 2002). The full text of the bill is available online at the Web site of the U.S. Department of Homeland Security: http://www.whitehouse.gov/deptofhomeland/bill/index.html#4 (accessed February 9, 2004).

33. http://www.whitehouse.gov/news/releases/2002/11/20021125-6.html (accessed March 17, 2004).

34. The recent amendment to the Medicare law is another example of this. Republicans released it a few days before the scheduled vote. The Republicans suggested that the bill must be passed immediately. They implied that there was no time for a thorough review, let alone a debate. After the bill became law, some members of both parties complained about not having "had the time" to deliberate. With the Republicans controlling the calendar, there may be little that opponents or more deliberative members can do to stop this runaway legislative train. Perhaps these members ought to refuse to vote and then explain the reasons to their constituents. It is better to not vote an ill-considered proposal into law than to regret it afterward, when the American people must bear the consequences.

35. John Gibeaut, "The Paperwork War on Terrorism," *American Bar Association Journal* 89 (October 2003): 63–68.

36. O'Harrow, Jr., "Six Weeks in Autumn."

CHAPTER 2 THE WAR IN THE COURTS

1. http://www.useu.be/Terrorism/USResponse/Sept1103USReportTerrorism.html (accessed March 10, 2004).

2. By November 2003 the Justice Department backed off of its claim that Moussaoui was the twentieth hijacker. See Susan Schmidt and Dan Eggen, "Al Qaeda Effort to Enter U.S. in August 2001 Reported," *Washington Post*, November 6, 2003. By then, two other people had been identified as hijackers, and Judge Brinkema ruled that she saw no evidence of his involvement in September 11.

3. Jerry Markon, "Major Issues in Moussaoui Appeal: Circuit Court Confronts Constitutional Questions in Terror Case," *Washington Post*, November 30, 2003.

4. Attorney General John Ashcroft (press conference, Washington, D.C., February 5, 2002). The text of the press conference is available online at the Web site of the U.S. Department of Justice: http://www.usdoj.gov/ag/speeches/2002/020502transcriptindict mentofjohnwalkerlindh.htm (accessed February 9, 2004).

5. The indictment is available online at the Web site of the U.S. Department of Justice: http://www.usdoj.gov/ag/2ndindictment.htm (accessed February 9, 2004).

6. Douglas Kmiec, "Try Lindh for Treason," *National Review Online*, January 21, 2002, http://www.nationalreview.com/comment/comment-kmiec012102.shtml (accessed March 10, 2004).

7. Bureau of International Information Programs, "White House Releases Progress Report on Global War on Terrorism," U.S. Department of State, September 10, 2003, http://usinfo.state.gov/topical/pol/terror/texts/03091009.htm (accessed February 9, 2004).

8. Matthew Purdy and Lowell Bergman, "Where the Trail Led: Between Evidence and Suspicion; Unclear Danger: Inside the Lackawanna Terror Case," *New York Times*, October 12, 2003, http://query.nytimes.com/gst/abstract.html?res=F10610FE385B0C718 DDDA90994DB404482 (accessed March 10, 2004); "Chasing the Sleeper Cell," *Frontline*, PBS, October 16, 2003.

9. Ibid.

10. "Ashcroft: New FBI Plan Protects Rights," Fox News.com, March 31, 2002, http://www.foxnews.com/story/0,2933,54115,00.html (accessed March 10, 2004).

11. George W. Bush, "State of the Union," January 28, 2003, http://www.whitehouse.gov/news/releases/2003/01/20030128-19.html (accessed March 10, 2004).

12. Michael Powell, "No Choice But Guilty; Lackawanna Case Highlights Legal Tilt," *Washington Post*, July 29, 2003.

13. Powell, "No Choice but Guilty."

14. Mark Fazlloh, "Mixed Verdict in First Terror Trial," *Philadelphia Inquirer*, June 4, 2003.

15. The statement of Jeffrey G. Collins, United States attorney, regarding the case of *United States v. Koubriti, et al.*, made on June 3, 2002, is available online at the Web site of the U.S. Department of Justice: http://www.usdoj.gov/usao/mie/pr/koubriti.html (accessed February 9, 2004).

16. Robert E. Pierre, "Terrorism Case Thrown into Turmoil, Factors Judge Is Considering Include Evidence Withheld from Defense," *Washington Post*, December 31, 2003.

17. Ibid.

18. "Ujaama's Guilty Plea Part of Deal to Testify Against Radical Cleric," September 19, 2003, http://seattletimes.nwsource.com/html/localnews/134675699_ujaama150.html (accessed September 19, 2003).

19. Associated Press, "Oregon Brothers Admit Conspiring to Help Al Qaeda, Taliban," *Washington Post*, September 19, 2003.

20. Andrew Kramer, "Two Sentenced for Trying to Join Taliban," Free Republic.com, November 24, 2003, http://209.157.64.200/focus/f-news/1028103/posts (accessed November 24, 2003).

21. Associated Press, "U.S. Woman Gets 3 Years for Plot to Aid Taliban," *Washington Post*, December 2, 2003.

22. Mary Beth Sheridan, "More Serious Charges Possible in 'Va. Jihad Network' Case," *Washington Post*, August 1, 2003, http://www.washingtonpost.com/ac2/wp-dyn/A13377-2003Aug1 (accessed August 1, 2003).

23. Jerry Markon, "3 Defendants Sentenced in Va. 'Jihad' Case," *Washington Post*, sec. B, 1. November 8, 2003.

24. Eric Lichtblau, "Trucker Sentenced to 20 Years in Plot Against Brooklyn Bridge," *New York Times*, October 29, 2003, http://www.nytimes.com/2003/10/29/national/29TERR.html (accessed October 29, 2003).

25. "Feds: Professor by Day, Terror Fund Raiser by Night; Lawyer: Indictment 'A Work of Fiction,'" *CNN.com*, http://www.cnn.com/2003/US/South/02/20/professor.background/index.html (accessed October 29, 2003).

26. Ibid.

27. Remarks to Financial Action Task Force, October 29, 2001, http://www.usdoj.gov/ag/speeches/2001/1029financialaction.htm (accessed March 10, 2004).

28. Vickie Chachere, "Judge Moves to Keep Evidence in Tampa Terror Case from Public," *Daytona Beach (FL) News Journal*, September 12, 2003, http://www.news-journalonline.com/cgi-bin/printme.asp (accessed October 29, 2003).

29. Dale Russakoff, "N.J. Judge Unseals Transcript in Controversial Terror Case, Lawyer Says Unraveled Charges Show Peril of Secret Evidence," *Washington Post*, June 25, 2003.

30. *Yaser Hamdi et al. v. Donald Rumsfeld et al.*, 296 F. 3d 278 (4th Cir. 2002). The full opinion is available online at FindLaw.com: http://news.findlaw.com/hdocs/docs/terrorism/hamdirums71202opn.pdf (accessed February 9, 2004).

31. *Jose Padilla v. Donald Rumsfeld*, Case Nos. 03-2235, 03-2483, (2nd Cir. 2003.) The full text of the opinion is available online at the Web site of the Center for Constitutional Rights: http://www.ccr-ny.org/v2/legal/september_11th/docs/PadillaCircuitDecision.pdf (accessed February 9, 2004).

32. Nat Hentoff, "Liberty's Court of Last Resort," *Village Voice*, January 24, 2003, http://www.villagevoice.com/issues/0305/hentoff.php (accessed March 10, 2004).

33. Ibid.

34. *Yaser Hamdi et al. v. Donald Rumsfeld et al.*, 296 F. 3d 278 (4th Circuit 2002).

35. Jerry Markon and Dan Eggen, "U.S. Allows Lawyer for Citizen Held as 'Enemy Combatant,'" *Washington Post*, December 3, 2003.

36. Editorial, "The Court's Conscience," *Washington Post*, October 10, 2003.

37. *Donald H. Rumsfeld v. Jose Padilla and Donna R. Newman*, Brief of the Cato Institute as Amicus Curiae in Support of Respondents (Case No. 03-1027), http://www.jenner.com/files/tbl_s69NewsDocumentOrder/FileUpload500/246/AmicusCuriae_Cato.pdf (accessed May 26, 2004).

38. Supreme Court Justice William Rehnquist, interview by David Gergen, *News Hour with Jim Lehrer*, PBS, November 11, 1998. The text of the interview is available online at the PBS Web site: http://www.pbs.org/newshour/gergen/november98/gergen_11-11.html (accessed November 24, 2003).

CHAPTER 3 THE WAR AGAINST LAWYERS

1. Prepared Remarks of Attorney General John Ashcroft, Islamic Group Indictment/ SAMs, April 2, 2002, online at www.fas.org/irp/news/2002/04/ag040902.html (accessed March 10, 2004). On October 31, 2001, the attorney general promulgated an amendment to 28 C.F.R. Parts 500 and 501, regulations directed at federal prison authorities, that became effective immediately without the usual opportunity for prior public comment.

2. For the text of the request for special confinement conditions, see the Web site of the U.S. Department of Justice: http://www.usdoj.gov/usao/eousa/foia_reading_room/usam/title9/24mcrm.htm.

3. Pursuant to 28 C.F.R. § 501.3, which became effective on May 17, 1996, the attorney general may authorize the director of the Bureau of Prisons (BOP) to implement Special Administrative Measures (SAMs) upon written notification to the BOP "that there is a substantial risk that a prisoner's communications or contacts with persons could result in death or serious bodily injury to persons, or substantial damage to property that would entail the risk of death or serious bodily injury to persons." The regulation provides that such notification to the BOP may be provided by the attorney general, "or at the attorney general's direction by the head of a federal law enforcement agency or the head of a member agency of the United States intelligence community." SAMs that ordinarily may be imposed "may include housing the inmate in administrative detention and/or limiting certain privileges, including, but not limited to, correspondence, visiting, interviews with representatives of the news media, and use of the telephone, as is reasonably necessary to protect persons against the risk of acts of violence or terrorism."

Although 28 C.F.R. § 501.3(a) allows *notification* to the BOP by the attorney general, or at the attorney general's discretion by the head of a federal law enforcement agency or the head of a member agency of the intelligence community, that an inmate's ability to communicate with other persons may create a substantial risk of death or serious bodily injury, only the attorney general is authorized to *direct* the BOP to implement the SAMs with respect to an inmate.

4. Prepared Remarks of Attorney General John Ashcroft, Islamic Group Indictment/SAMs, April 9, 2002, http://www.fas.org/irp/news/2002/04/ag040902.html (accessed March 17, 2003).

5. Dave Lindorff, "Defense Lawyer or Terrorist's Accomplice?" *Salon.com*, August 2, 2002, http://www.salon.com/news/feature/2002/08/02/stewart/index_np.html (accessed February 9, 2004).

6. The full text of Lindh's plea agreement is available online at FindLaw.com: http://news.findlaw.com/cnn/docs/terrorism/uslindh71502pleaag.pdf (accessed February 9, 2004).

7. Jesselyn Raddack, personal communication by phone with author, September 14, 2003.

8. Senator Edward M. Kennedy of Massachusetts, speaking at the Judiciary Committee executive business meeting regarding the nomination of Michael Chertoff to the United States Court of Appeals for the Third Circuit, March 23, 2003. The texts of his comments are available online at the Web site of the Reporters Committee for Freedom of the Press: http://www.rcfp.org/behindthehomefront/docs/pr_kennedy.html (accessed September 14, 2003).

9. Stephen Kenny, interview by Leigh Sales, Australian Broadcasting Company News, December 18, 2003, http://www.abc.net.au/am/content/2003/s1012448.htm (accessed March 10, 2004).

10. Dan Eggen, "Audio of Attorney-Detainee Interviews Called Illegal," *Washington Post*, December 20, 2003.

CHAPTER 4 GUILT BY ASSOCIATION

1. Secretary Paul O'Neill remarks on next terrorist asset list, "O'Neill Reports Progress Against Terrorist Financing," http://usinfo.state.gov/topical/pol/terror/02010908.htm (accessed March 10, 2004).

2. http://usinfo.state.gov/regional/nea/summit/text2003/0615pwl.htm (accessed March 10, 2004).

3. Statement of the Attorney General, Indictments, February 20, 2003, http://www.usdoj.gov/ag/speeches/2003/02202003pressconference.htm (accessed March 10, 2004).

4. Remarks by President on Financial Fight Against Terror, December 4, 2001, http://www.whitehouse.gov/news/releases/2001/12/20011204-8.html (accessed March 10, 2004).

5. For a good discussion of this law, see David Cole, *Enemy Aliens: Double Standards and Constitutional Freedoms in the War on Terrorism* (New York: New Press, 2003), 76–77. The International Emergency Economic Powers Act (IEEPA) amended the Trading with the Enemy Act (TWEA), which was passed in 1977 and gave virtually unlimited power to the president during war or a national emergency to regulate or prohibit foreign trade and international credit transactions. The TWEA was amended to authorize presidential action only during war, with the IEEPA becoming a repository for executive economic power wielded during other emergencies. The IEEPA also restricts the emergency powers to apply to international transactions only. For more details see Robert Higgs and Charlotte Twight, "National Emergency and Private Property Rights: Historical Relations and Present Conditions," Independent Institute, September 1986, http://www.independent.org/tii/news/860900Higgs.html.

6. Gregory L. Vistica, "Frozen Assets Going to Legal Bills: U.S. Has Linked Confiscated Funds to Financing Terror," *Washington Post*, November 1, 2003, http://www.washingtonpost.com/ac2/wp-dyn/A49038-2003Oct31 (accessed November 1, 2003).

7. OMB Watch, "The USA Patriot Act and its Impact on Nonprofit Organizations," September 10, 2003, http://www.ombwatch.org/article/articleview/1803/1/3 (accessed February 10, 2004).

8. The Center for Constitutional Rights (CCR) has been at the forefront of challenges to the laws, both before and after September 11, bringing actions in the names of political organizations such as the Humanitarian Law Project. See Nancy Chang and David Cole, *"Humanitarian Law Project, et al., v. John Ashcroft et al.,"* Center for Constitutional Rights, http://www.ccr-ny.org/v2/legal/govt_misconduct/govtArticle.asp?ObjID=FoF9XFivgG&Content=70.

9. These terms are used in the guilty pleas of the Lackawanna Six, concerning their attendance at an al Qaeda training camp; see chapter 2.

10. *Humanitarian Law Project, et al., v. Department of Justice, et al.*, Case No. CV 98-01971-ABC, decided December 3, 2003. The decision is available online at the Web site of the Court of Appeals for the Ninth Circuit: http://www.ca9.uscourts.gov/ca9/newopinions.nsf/044DE357BD726D7288256DF10063BDE4/$file/0255082.pdf?openelement (accessed February 9, 2004).

11. Center for Constitutional Rights, "Federal Appeals Court Declares Key Provisions of Anti-Terrorism Statute Unconstitutional," (press release, December 3, 2003), http://www.ccr-ny.org/v2/newsroom/releases/pReleases.asp?ObjID=NVUclM1aT7&Content=307 (accessed April 28, 2004).

12. December 18, 2002, http://www.useu.be/Terrorism/ECONNews/Dec1802US IndictsFinanceTerrorists.html (accessed March 10, 2004).

13. "Bush Targets Hamas Money," December 4, 2001, CBS News.com, http://www.cbsnews.com/stories/2001/12/04/attack/main320009.shtml. (accessed March 10, 2004).

14. December 18, 2002, http://www.useu.be/Terrorism/ECONNews/dec1802US IndictsFinanceTerrorists.html (accessed March 10, 2004).

15. *Holy Land Foundation for Relief and Development v. Ashcroft*, 333 F.3d 156 (DC Cir. 2003).

16. ACLU, "Federal Appeals Court Declares Secret Deportation Hearings Unconstitutional in ACLU Victory," August 26, 2002, http://archive.aclu.org/news/2002/n082602a.html (accessed February 10, 2004).

17. Prepared remarks of Attorney General John Ashcroft, October 9, 2002, http://www.usdoj.gov/ag/speeches/2002/100902agremarksbifindictment.htm (accessed March 10, 2004).

18. Andrew Purvis, "Money Trouble," *Time Europe*, July 1, 2002, http://www.time.com/time/europe/magazine/printout/0,13155,901020701-265360,00.html (accessed October 24, 2003).

19. "Benevolence Director Pleads Guilty to Racketeering Conspiracy and Agrees to Cooperate with Government," press release, U.S. Department of Justice, February 10, 2002, http://216.239.41.104/search?q=cache:MpZU-caUAKsJ:www.usdoj.gov/usao/iln/pr/2003/pr021003_01.pdf+Arnaout%2Bsentence&hl=en&ie=UTF-8 (accessed March 10, 2004).

20. "Muslim Charity Leader Sentenced to 11 Years," Islamic Broadcasting News. com, August 18, 2003, http://news.ibn.net/newsgen.asp?url=cahrilesen (accessed March 10, 2004).

21. Douglas Farah, "Terror Probe Points to Va. Muslims," *Washington Post*, sec. A, October 18, 2003.

22. Ibid.

23. Douglas Farah, "U.S. Links Islamic Charities, Terrorist Funding," *Washington Post*, August 20, 2003, http://www.washingtonpost.com/wp-dyn/articles/A17354-2003Aug19.html.

24. Jerry Markon, "Man Convicted in Islamic Charity Probe," *Washington Post*, October 10, 2003.

25. Josh White, "Virginia Terror Suspect Sentenced to 1 Year, Man Guilty of Lying to Get Citizenship," *Washington Post*, January 13, 2004.

26. The indictment is available online at FindLaw.com: http://news.findlaw.com/hdocs/docs/terrorism/usalamoudi102303ind.pdf (accessed February 10, 2004).

27. Douglas Farah and John Mintz, "U.S. Charges Activist Over Links to Libya," *Washington Post*, September 30, 2003.

28. The first indictment against Alamoudi came a few days after the highly publicized detention of army chaplain James Yee, prison chaplain for detainees in Guantanamo Bay, Cuba. (Yee himself was first alleged to have been engaging in espionage against the United States in support of terrorism. In December, the charges against him were reduced to downloading pornography on his government computer and committing adultery with a fellow officer.)

29. Mary Beth Sheridan and Douglas Farah, "Jailed Muslim Had Made a Name in Washington," *Washington Post*, sec. 4, December 1, 2003.

30. Douglas Farah, "U.S. Indicts Prominent Muslim Here," *Washington Post*, October 24, 2003, http://www.philly.com/mld/journalgazette/news7093854.htm (accessed March 10, 2004).

31. Douglas Farah, "Terror Probe Points to Va. Muslims," *Washington Post*, October 18, 2003, www.washingtonpost.com/ac2/wpdyn?pagename=article&node=&contented=A43559-2003Oct17&notFound=true (accessed March 10, 2004).

32. February 13, 2003 Indictment, http://news/findlaw/com/hdocs/docs/ins/usalhussayen21303ind.pdf (accessed March 10, 2004).

33. Susan Schmidt, "5 Tied to Islamic Charity Indicted in N.Y., Idaho," *Washington Post*, February 27, 2003, www.washingtonpost.com/ac2/wp-dyn/A8329-2003Feb26 (accessed October 24, 2003). Susan Schmidt, "U.S. Indicts Saudi Student, Internet Allegedly Used to Aid Terrorist Groups in Jihad," *Washington Post*, January 10, 2004.

34. "The Status of Muslim Civil Rights in the United States, 2002: Sterotypes and Civil Liberties," http://www.cair-net.org/civilrights2002/civilrights2002.doc (accessed March 10, 2004).

35. Personal phone communication, September 14, 2002.

36. No author, Beloit Daily News.com, "Charity Leader Charged with Racketeering," October 10, 2002, www.beloitdailynews.com/1002/3ill10.htm (accessed March 10, 2004).

CHAPTER 5 SEIZURES, DETENTIONS, AND DEPORTATIONS

1. http://judiciary.senate.gov/testimony.cfm?id=121&wit_id=42.

2. David Cole, *Enemy Aliens*, 172.

3. "Deportation of Professor Cost at Least $138,995," *Naples* (FL) *News*, September 3, 2003.

4. Dan Herbeck, "U.S. Drops Two Charges Against Algerian," *Buffalo* (NY) *News*, October 10, 2003.

5. See chap. 1, note 12.

6. "Ashcroft Wants Broader Anti-Terror Powers," *Washington Post*, June 5, 2003, http://www.washingtonpost.com/wp-dyn/articles/A19458-2003Jun5.html (accessed June 5, 2003).

7. *Detroit Free Press v. Ashcroft*, 303 F. 3d 691, 683 (6th Cir. 2002).

8. Ibid.

9. Dan Christensen, "Scrutinizing 'Supersealed' Cases: Judges, Lawyers Question Secrecy Surrounding Case Linked to Terrorism Probes," *Miami Daily Business Review*, December 2, 2003, http://www.law.com/jsp/article.jsp?id=1069801668123 (accessed April 28, 2004).

10. David Cole, *Enemy Aliens*, 162.

11. R. Jeffrey Smith, "Patriot Act Used in 16-Year-Old Deportation Case," *Washington Post*, September 23, 2003.

12. Robert E. Pierre, "Palestinian Activist Is Released," *Washington Post*, November 4, 2003.

13. David Cole, "9/11 and the LA 8," *The Nation*, October 9, 2003, http://www.thenation.com/doc.mhtml?i=20031027&s=cole (accessed February 10, 2004).

14. Stanton and Bazar, "Security Collides with Civil Liberties" (see intro, note 3).

15. Maher Arar, "The Put a Bag Over My Head and Flew Me to Syria for Torture and Interrogation," *CounterPunch*, November 6, 2003, http://www.counterpunch.org/arar11062003.html (accessed March 11, 2004).

16. DeNeen L. Brown and Dana Priest, "Deported Terror Suspect Details Torture in Syria," *Washington Post*, November 5, 2003.

17. Carlyle Murphy and John Mintz, "Virginia Man's Months in Saudi Prison Go Unexplained," *Washington Post*, November 22, 2003, http://www.washingtonpost.com/ac2/wp-dyn/A4967-2003Nov21 (accessed November 22, 2003).

18. Ibid.

19. *Shafiq Rasul et al., v. George W. Bush, et al.*, (Case Nos. 03-334 and 03-343), on petitions for a writ of certiorari to the United States Court of Appeals for the District of Columbia, Brief for the Respondents in Opposition, http://news.findlaw/com/cnn/docs/scotus/rasulodahoct03sgopbrf.html (accessed March 11, 2004).

20. Charles Lane, "Supreme Court Revisits Enemy Combatants," *Washington Post*, November 23, 2003.

21. *Shafiq Rasul et al., v. George W. Bush, et al.*, (Case Nos. 03-334 and 03-343), on petitions for a writ of certiorari to the United States Court of Appeals for the District of Columbia, Amicus Brief of Amicus Curiae Fred Korematsu in Support of Petitioners, http://www.appellate.net/guantanamo_bay/Fred_Korematsu_amicusbrief0104.pdf (accessed March 11, 2004).

CHAPTER 6 POPULAR RESISTANCE IN THE WAR ON CIVIL LIBERTIES

1. Mike Rster, "Plans and Goals," Libertarian Party of Alabama, http://www.al.lp.org/issues/patriotactresistance.htm (accessed November 29, 2003).

2. Amy Goldstein, "Fierce Fight Over Secrecy, Scope of the Law," *Washington Post*, September 8, 2003.

3. Curt Anderson, "Ashcroft to Declassify Data Showing How Often Government Has Sought Library Records," *Washington Post*, September 17, 2003.

4. Chicago, Illinois Resolution, http://www.aclu.org/SafeandFree/SafeandFree.cfm?ID=13882&c=207 (accessed March 11, 2004).

5. Amanda Klonsky and Noah Leavitt, "What's a Nice Jewish Activist Like You Doing in a City Council Meeting: How Chicago's Jewish and Muslim Communities Came Together to Fight the PATRIOT Act (and Won!)," http://www.jcua.org/socialaction_article.pdf (accessed March 11, 2004).

6. Noah Leavitt, "The USA PATRIOT Act: Bad for Jews, Bad for Immigrants, Bad for Americans," http://www.jcua.org/patriotact.pdf (accessed March 11, 2004).

7. Fran Spellman, "Council Decries Patriot Act in Watered-Down Resolution," *Chicago Sun-Times*, October 3, 2003, http://Chicago.indymedia.org/newswire/display/31419 (accessed March 11, 2004).

8. Grass Roots America Defends the Bill of Rights (press release, October 23, 2003).

9. Charlie Norwood, "Statement: The CLEAR Act of 2003," Numbers USA, July 9, 2003, http://www.numbersusa.com/hottopic/clearact.html (accessed October 23, 2003).

10. "Clear Act Could Produce Racial Profiling by Police Officers," *Desert Sun* (Palm Springs, CA), October 19, 2003, http://www.thedesertsun.com/news/stories2003/opinion/20031019035832.shtml (accessed October 19, 2003).

11. ACLU, "The ACLU in the Courts since 9/11," http://www.aclu.org/SafeandFree/SafeandFree.cfm?ID=11779&c=207 (accessed March 11, 2004).

12. *Detroit Free Press v. Ashcroft*, 303 F. 3d 691, 683 (6th Cir. 2002).

13. Mark Hamblett, "Prosecutors Win Big in Terrorism Ruling," *New York Law Journal* (November 10, 2003), http://www.law.com/jsp/article.jsp?id=1067351008834 (accessed November 10, 2003).

14. Sara B. Miller and Seth Stern, "Odd Bedfellows Fall in Line," *Christian Science Monitor*, October 29, 2003, http://www.csmonitor.com/2003/1029/p16s01-usju.html (accessed October 29, 2003).

15. Michael Moore, "Patriot Act: What It Is," http://www.michaelmoore.com/takeaction/issues/patriotact.php (accessed March 11, 2004). William Safire, "You Are a Suspect," *New York Times*, November 14, 2002, http://truthout.com/docs_02/11.16F.safire.you.htm (accessed March 11, 2004).

16. Audrey Hudson, "Senators Join Forces to Roll Back Parts of Patriot Act," *Washington Times*, October 16, 2003.

17. Jerry Seper, "Revised SAFE Act May Spur Veto," *Washington Times*, January 29, 2004, http://www.washtimes.com/national/20040129-115041-5491r.htm.

18. President George W. Bush, "State of the Union 2004," January 20, 2004, http://www.whitehouse.gov/stateoftheunion/2004 (accessed March 11, 2004).

CHAPTER 7 A WAR WITHOUT END

1. President George W. Bush, "State of the Union 2004," January 20, 2004, http://www.whitehouse.gov/stateoftheunion/2004 (accessed March 11, 2004).

2. John V. Whitbeck, "'Terrorism': A World Ensnared by a Word," *International Herald Tribune*, February 18, 2004, http://www.commondreams.org/views04/0218-12.htm (accessed March 11, 2004).

3. Personal conversation with the author, Washington, D.C., October 7, 2003.

4. David Cole, "Analysis of Immigration and Fund-Raising Provisions in Omnibus Counterterrorism Act of 1995," http://www.cpsr.org/cpsr/privacy/epic/cole_analysis_antiterrorism.html (accessed March 17, 2004).

5. "Bush Says It Is Time for Action," CNN, November 6, 2001, http://www.cnn.com/2001/US/11/06/ret.bush.coalition/index.html (accessed March 11, 2004).

6. The terrorism charges backfired, so to speak, on the prosecutors when judges in both cases agreed with defense attorneys that if the community was a victim, then it could

not be the source of an impartial jury pool. This led both trials being moved several hundred miles from the D.C. area.

7. Dean Schabner, "Target: 'Narco-Terror': Draft Bill Would Provide Broader Power,: ABC News, August 20, 2003, http://abcnews.go.com/sections/us/WorldNewsTonight/victory_act030820.html (accessed March 11, 2004).

8. C-Span, Washington Journal, March 15, 2004.

9. Charles Piller, "A Trying Time for Science," *Los Angeles Times*, October 28, 2003, http://www.latimes.com/news/science/la-sci-butler28oct28002420,1,296622.story?coll=la-news-science (accessed October 28, 2003).

10. http://www.nti.org/d_newswire/issues/2003/10/28/e9cc7ace-84f7-4091-a46b-23f77d216c07.html.

11. (GAO-03-266), http://www.rcfp.org/news/2003/0221gao032.html.

12. Eric Lichtblau, "U.S. Uses Terror Law to Pursue Crimes from Drugs to Swindling," *New York Times*, September 27, 2003, reproduced at http://www.globalpolicy.org/wtc/liberties/2003/0927swindling.htm (accessed March 11, 2004). Government Accounting Office, Major Management Challenges and Program Risks: Department of Justice (GAO-03-105), January 1, 2003, online at http://www.gao.gov/atext/d03105.txt (accessed March 11, 2004).

13. Code of Federal Regulations, title 31, part 103 (2002). The full text of the regulation, 31 C.F.R. Part 103, can be accessed online through a link at Investment Company Institute, "Treasury Proposes Rules to Implement PATRIOT Act," January 8, 2002, http://www.ici.org/issues/fserv/arc-reg/02_treas_aml_interim.html.

14. For a full account of the FBI's visit to Cryptome, see Cryptome's Web site at http://cryptome.org/fbi-cryptome.htm.

15. International Studies in Higher Education Act of 2003, HR 3077, 108th Congress, 1st session, *Congressional Record*, October 21, 2003, H 9753.

16. "Defunct Big Brother Spying Program Resurfaces as 'Little Brother' in Seven States," October 30, 2003, http://www.aclu.org/Privacy/Privacy.cfm?ID=14257&c=130 (accessed February 13, 2004).

17. Associated Press, "Georgia Stayed in Matrix Database Despite Governor's Statement It Was Withdrawing," *Atlanta Journal Constitution*, January 30, 2004, http://www.ajc.com/metro/content/metro/0104/30matrix.html (accessed February 13, 2004).

18. President George W. Bush, "State of the Union 2004," January 20, 2004, http://www.whitehouse.gov/stateoftheunion/2004 (accessed March 11, 2004).

19. ACLU, "Insatiable Appetite: The Government's Demand for New and Unnecessary Powers After September 11," April 2002, http://archive.aclu.org/congress/InsatiableAppetite.pdf (accessed September 27, 2003).

20. Ann Coulter, *Treason*, New York: Crown Forum, 2003.

21. David Cole, personal meeting with author, Georgetown University Law School, October 7, 2003.

22. Ibid.

23. These views were expressed by attorney Ashraf Nubani, personal communication with author, October 9, 2003.

24. Josef Joffe, "Locking Out the Brainpower," *Washington Post*, November 23, 2003. Joffee notes that at the height of the technology boom, one-fourth of Silicon Valley's high-tech firms were headed by executives of Chinese and Indian descent.

25. "Going After Criminals," *Buffalo* (NY) *News*, October 10, 2003, http://www.buffalonews.com (accessed October 10, 2003).

26. Stanley Cohen, lecture, Portland State University, August 27, 2003. The text of this lecture is available online at the Web site of the Portland Independent Media Center: http://portland.indymedia.org/en/2003/08/270707.shtml (accessed August 28, 2003).

27. David Cole, *Enemy Aliens*.

28. Gore Vidal, *Perpetual War for Perpetual Peace* (New York: Thunder's Mouth Press/ Nation Books, 2002).

29. *Ellen Mariani vs. George W. Bush, et al.* (Case No. 03-5273), U.S. District Court for the Eastern District of Pennsylvania. Case is still pending. The text of the amended bill of complaint is available online at www.911timeline.net/marianivsbush.htm (accessed February 12, 2004).

30. http://www.msnbc.msn.com/id/4179618 (accessed March 11, 2004).

31. http://www.cnn.com/2004/ALLPOLITICS/03/03/eleco4.prez.bush.ads/index.html (accessed April 28, 2004).

32. Brent Scowcroft, "Don't Attack Saddam," *Wall Street Journal*, August 2, 2002, http://www.j-bradford-delong.net/movable_type/archives/000504.html (accessed February 13, 2004).

33. http://www.cnn.com/2002/US/12/17/ashcroft.terror.rights/ (accessed March 11, 2004).

AFTERWORD

1. Mike Allen, "President Campaigns to Make Patriot Act Permanent," *Washington Post*, April 20, 2004.

2. www.aclu.org/SafeandFree/SafeandFree.cfm?ID=15525&c=206 (accessed April 26, 2004).

3. "Latest Provision of Patriot 2 Comes Before House Subcommittee," www.aclu.org/SafeandFree/SafeandFree.cfm?ID=15517&c=206 (accessed April 26, 2004).

4. "Britain Frees 5 Citizens Sent Home from U.S. Jail," Reuters, *New York Times*, March 11, 2004, www.nytimes.com/2004/03/11/international/Europe/11GITM.html (accessed March 13, 2004).

5. John Mintz and Robin Wright, "Spanish Detainee Sent Home," *Washington Post*, February 12, 2004.

6. Pamela Constable, "An Afghan Boy's Life in U.S. Custody," *Washington Post*, February 12, 2004.

7. Neil A. Lewis and Eric Schmitt, "Detainees Facing Years in Cuba Brig," *New York Times*, February 14, 2004.

8. "U.S. May Hold Cleared Detainees," *BBC News*, February 27, 2004, http://news. bbc.co.uk (accessed March 4, 2004).

9. Vernon Loeb, "Panel Set Up To Hear Pleas of Detainees; Rumsfeld: Cuba Prisoners Will Get Annual Reviews," *Washington Post*, February 14, 2004.

10. Matthew Barakat, "Three Found Guilty in Virginia Jihad Case," *Washington Post*, March 4, 2004, http://www.washingtonpost.com/wp-dyn/articles/A30709-2004Mar4. html (accessed March 4, 2004).

11. Personal e-mail from Nubani to author, March 4, 2004.

12. Jerry Markon, "Moussaoui Lawyers Heartened by Appeal Court's Reasoning," *Washington Post*, April 24, 2004.

13. "Seattle-Raised Muslim Convert Sentenced Friday, Feb. 13," Nation in Brief, *Washington Post*, February 15, 2004.

14. Nation in Brief, *Washington Post*, February 10, 2004.

15. Associated Press, "Detroit Case Federal Prosecutor Sues Ashcroft, Suit Accuses Justice Department of Mismanaging War on Terrorism," *Washington Post*, February 17, 2004, www.washingtonpost.com/ac2/wp-dyn/A47812-2004Feb17 (accessed February 17, 2004).

16. Personal e-mail from Radack to author, March 2, 2004.

17. Jesselyn Radack, "Broken Wings: The Indignities of Being on the No-Fly List," April 15, 2004, *Civil Liberties Watch*, http://babelogue.citypages.com:8080/ecassel/ (accessed April 15, 2004).

18. John Burgess, "German Court Overturns Sept. 11 Conviction," *Washington Post*, March 4, 2004, http://www.washingtonpost.com/wp-dyn/articles/A29401-2004Mar4.html (accessed March 4, 2004).

19. Associated Press. "Texas Professor Gets Two-Year Prison Term in Plague Case." *Washington Post*, March 11, 2004.

20. Michael Powell, "Lawyer Visits 'Dirty Bomb' Suspect," *Washington Post*, March 4, 2004, http://www.washingtonpost.com/wp-dyn/articles/A28390-2004Mar3.html (accessed March 4, 2004).

21. "Ex-professor Was FBI Informant," CNN.com, April 6, 2004, www.cnn.com/ 2004/LAW/04/06/attacks.professor.ap (accessed April 6, 2004).

22. Sara Kehaulani Goo, "Report Faults TSA On Privacy," *Washington Post*, February 13, 2004.

23. Mary Beth Sheridan, "Financial Agencies Criticize U.S. for Detaining Spanish IMF Worker at Dulles," *Washington Post*, March 11, 2003.

24. E-mail of Segura and Alvey, http://www.dr5.org/mt/archives/000465.html.

25. "Staff Statement No. 10: Threats and Responses in 2001," Staff Statement No. 10, www.9-11commission.gov/hearings/hearing10/staff_statement_10.pdf (accessed April 26, 2004).

26. "Homeland Security Memo," *Washington Post*, Style, February 10, 2004.

27. Jeff Eckhoff and Mark Siebert, "U.S. Officials Drop Activist Subpoenas," *Des Moines (IA) Register*, February 11, 2004, http://desmoinesregister.com/news/stories/c4788993/23504845.html (accessed February 11, 2004).

28. Eric Lichtblau, "F.B.I. Scrutinizes Antiwar Rallies," *New York Times*, November 23, 2003, online at www.commondreams.org/headlines03/1122-09.htm (accessed March 13, 2004).

29. Jennifer Kimmitt, "Retired Georgia State Professor on Trial for Antiwar Protests," *Georgia State University Signal*, March 2, 2004, http://www.gsusignal.com/vnews/display.v/ART/2004/03/02/4044ff113a61d (accessed March 4, 2004).

30. Emma Graves Fitzsimmons, "Army Inquiries Alarm Students at U. Texas," *Daily Texan* (University of Texas-Austin), February 17, 2004, http://www.bupipedream.com/021704/wire/w2.htm (accessed March 13, 2004). As to Chicago, Robert Dreyfuss, "The Watchful and the Wary," *Mother Jones*, July-August, 2003, http://www.findarticles.com/cf_dls/m1329/4_28/104652226/pl/article.jhtml (accessed March 13, 2004).

31. "Civil Liberties Safe Zones," Bill of Rights Defense Committee, www.bordc.org (accessed April 26, 2004).

32. Kim Zetter, "The Patriot Act Is Your Friend," *Wired*, February 24, 2004, http://www.wired.com/news/politics/0,1283,62388-2,00.html?tw=wn_story_page_next2 (accessed March 3, 2004).

33. Adam Liptak, "The Crime of Editing, U.S. Tells Publishers Not to Touch a Comma in Manuscript from Iran," *New York Times*, February 28, 2004, http://query.nytimes.com/gst/abstract.html?res=F50F11F835580C7B8EDDAB0894DC404482 (accessed March 13, 2004).

34. Nation in Brief, *Washington Post*, April 25, 2004.

35. Dan Froomkin, "Bush Goes on Background," *Washington Post*, March 3, 2004, http://www.washingtonpost.com/wp-dyn/articles/A26077-2004Mar3.html (accessed March 13, 2004).